The 100 Most Jewish Foods

The 100 MOST JEWISH FOODS

A Highly Debatable List

Edited by **Alana Newhouse**
With **Stephanie Butnick**

Photographs by Noah Fecks
Illustrations by Joana Avillez
Recipe editing by Gabriella Gershenson

Artisan | New York

Library of Congress Cataloging-in-Publication Data

Names: Newhouse, Alana, editor. | Avillez, Joana, illustrator.
Title: The 100 most Jewish foods : a highly debatable list / edited by Alana
    Newhouse ; with Stephanie Butnick ; photographs by Noah Fecks ; recipe editing
    by Gabriella Gershenson; illustrations by Joana Avillez.
Other titles: The one hundred most Jewish foods
Description: New York : Artisan, a division of Workman Publishing Co., Inc.
    [2019] | Includes index.
Identifiers: LCCN 2018047571 | ISBN 9781579659066 (hardcover : alk. paper)
Subjects: LCSH: Jewish cooking. | LCGFT: Cookbooks.
Classification: LCC TX724 .A23 2019 | DDC 641.5/676—dc23
LC record available at https://lccn.loc.gov/2018047571

Creative direction by Michelle Ishay-Cohen
Design by Raphael Geroni
Cover lettering by Kimberly Glyder

Artisan books are available at special discounts when purchased in bulk for premiums
and sales promotions as well as for fund-raising or educational use. Special editions or
book excerpts also can be created to specification. For details, contact the Special Sales
Director at the address below, or send an e-mail to specialmarkets@workman.com.

For speaking engagements, contact speakersbureau@workman.com.

Published by Artisan
A division of Workman Publishing Co., Inc.
225 Varick Street
New York, NY 10014-4381
artisanbooks.com

Artisan is a registered trademark of Workman Publishing Co., Inc.

Published simultaneously in Canada by Thomas Allen & Son, Limited

Printed in Canada

First printing, February 2019

10 9 8 7 6 5 4 3 2 1

FOR MY GRANDMOTHER, AND YOURS

CONTENTS

Kishke · **158**

Kosher Salt · **160**

Kosher Sushi · **162**

Kreplach · **163**

Kubbeh · **166**

Kugel · **171**

Labda · **173**

Lamb (Not the Leg. And
Definitely Not Roasted.) · **176**

Leftovers · **180**

Lox · **182**

Macaroons · **185**

Malida · **188**

Margarine · **191**

Matzo · **193**

Matzo Balls · **195**

Matzo Brei · **198**

Mina de Matzo · **201**

Mufleta · **205**

Olives · **210**

Pareve Chocolate · **212**

Persian Rice · **214**

Pickles · **216**

Pkaila · **220**

Pomegranates · **223**

Poppy Seeds · **224**

Potatoes · **226**

Ptcha · **228**

Rye Bread · **230**

INTRODUCTION

Sigmund Freud once said, "Jews and food; food and Jews—that's all there is."

OK, not exactly. But after putting together this unfathomably rich collection—the salty, the sweet, the dense, the light, the beautiful, and the undeniably brown, stretching back over thousands of years of civilization and from nearly every region of the planet—we believe the great neurologist and father of psychoanalysis would agree with us: It is quite possible to view all of human history as unfolding between these two poles.

This is not a list of today's most popular Jewish foods, or someone's idea of the tastiest, or even the most enduring. In fact, a number of the dishes on this list are no longer cooked or served with any regularity—at least not in the home kitchens or communal spaces where they originated—and the edibility of many others is . . . well, let's say it's up for debate.

What's here, instead, are the foods that contain the deepest Jewish significance—the ones that, through the history of our people (however you date it), have been most profoundly inspired by the rhythms of the Jewish calendar and the contingencies of the Jewish experience. That many of them are also delicious is obvious, and Darwinian: It's how they've survived as long as they have.

Most of the items on this list will be immediately recognizable: No one was going to leave out chicken soup or babka or *shakshuka* or . . . matzo. But there are also dishes here that, for many, won't be familiar at all: unhatched chicken eggs and jellied calves' feet, as well as recipes from around the globe and ones nearly lost to history. These are foods that were generated by a people that became many peoples; a tribe at once bound together by a shared tradition and separated by radically different host countries, cultures, politics, and influences. We found inspiration in this tension between what is shared and what is not.

When a version of this list appeared on *Tablet*'s website in early 2018, we were excited and moved by the overwhelming response. In this book, we've incorporated the energy of the conversation that followed, as well as taken on the one challenge posed to us by more readers than we could count: adding recipes. (It was a stressful undertaking: *You* try implying there is only one "right" way to make matzo brei.) We're proud to present this near encyclopedic collection of Jewish foods, with the hope that you'll not only reminisce about the various items on the list but also feel empowered to weave some new ones into your own traditions.

In addition to *Tablet* writers and editors, contributors include leading chefs and food writers: Éric Ripert on gefilte fish ("It's not as bad as it's made out to be!"); Gail Simmons on full-sour dill pickles ("the single most important food in my life"); Marcus Samuelsson's meditation on growing up eating lox in Sweden; Tom Colicchio on whitefish ("the redheaded stepchild of lox"); Melissa Clark on the primacy of the black-and-white cookie in New York City's robust Jewish cookie scene; and more.

Joan Nathan declares, "No Jewish dish is as comforting or iconic as the matzo ball"; Michael Solomonov calls traditional American noodle kugel "a shitty representation of Jewish food"; Dan Barber inhabits the perspective of the apple, from its exile from the Garden of Eden to our Rosh Hashanah tables; Yotam Ottolenghi bemoans the Hanukkah jelly doughnut, filled with a "gummy red jam that hasn't seen a single berry in its life"; and Food52's Amanda Hesser and Merrill Stubbs lament that WASPs like them grow up eating pot roast instead of brisket.

Also featured in these pages are writers and artists and thinkers. Maira Kalman calls herring the ultimate Jewish fish, Joshua Malina composes an ode to *gribenes* ("the kosher version of pork rinds"), and Action Bronson pays tribute to the Jewish affinity for Chinese food. Daphne Merkin praises Sweet'N Low, Shalom Auslander is traumatized by cholent, and Dr. Ruth Westheimer explains why pomegranates are sexy.

We aren't all food experts or cooks, and we aren't even all people who love the dishes we're writing about. It's an unexpected collection of contributors, and sometimes the people are even more interesting than the subjects themselves. By which we mean: The list is a lot like Jewish life.

With that, there's only one thing left to say: Enjoy.

Alana Newhouse
Founder and editor in chief, *Tablet*

Adafina

By David Gitlitz *and* Linda Davidson

Conversos and *confesos* were the prime terms applied in Iberia to Jews who converted to Christianity, willingly or under duress. While many converts assimilated into the Christian religion and culture, others strove to hang on to their Jewish identity. The Inquisition used remnant Jewish practices as a key to identifying the New Christians who still Judaized. Reports that certain people avoided pork and scaleless fish, soaked and salted their meat to remove the blood, dug out the sinew from their legs of lamb (page 176), or ate matzo and charoset around Easter time led inquisitors to arrest and interrogate the Judaizers.

The dish that figures most frequently in accounts of accusations by neighbors, friends, and servants is Sabbath stew. The ingredients—chunks of fish or cubes of lamb or beef (or, in the poorer families, root vegetables like beets or turnips, or perhaps cabbage), but never pork or shellfish—were entirely ordinary. They did not include tomatoes, potatoes, corn, or today's wide variety of squashes and peppers, because those were New World foods not yet popular in Europe.

Friday afternoon in a Judaizing *converso* kitchen, the women chopped, sliced, and braised the ingredients—always in olive oil rather than lard—while trying to deflect their servants' queries about why they weren't flavoring the pot with *tocino*, Iberia's ubiquitous salt pork. They added seasonal greens from the garden, and these varied by region. Wealthy families might add a dash of pepper; more humble folk might use the thyme, oregano, mint, or fennel that grew wild along every roadside. Once assembled, the ingredients were placed in an iron pot and a coil of bread dough was wrapped around the lid to seal in the flavors. The pot was put in a banked fire, the top covered with embers, and left overnight.

For inquisitors, the fact that the stews were prepared on Friday afternoon and eaten communally on Saturday was telling. The dish went by several names: *trasnochado* (Spanish for "overnighted"), *hamin* (from the Hebrew for "warm"), and *adafina* (Arabic for "hidden").

→

NEW-WORLD ADAFINA

Serves 6 to 8

FOR THE ADAFINA SAUCE

6 cups (1.4 liters) vegetable stock or water

1 tablespoon (15 grams) kosher salt, plus more as needed

2 teaspoons ground cumin

1½ teaspoons smoked paprika

1 teaspoon sweet paprika

1 teaspoon onion powder

1 teaspoon garlic powder

½ teaspoon red pepper flakes or cayenne pepper (optional)

¼ teaspoon ground cinnamon

¼ teaspoon freshly ground black pepper

FOR THE ADAFINA

2 tablespoons (30 milliliters) olive oil

1 large yellow onion, chopped

1 cup (185 grams) dried chickpeas, soaked in cold water overnight and drained

1½ teaspoons kosher salt, plus more as needed

1 cup (195 grams) dried pinto or kidney beans, soaked in cold water overnight and drained

1 cup (200 grams) barley or wheat berries

1 pound (455 grams) baby potatoes (about 20), halved if large

1 pound (455 grams) sweet potatoes (about 2 medium), peeled and cut into large chunks

4¼ ounces (125 grams) pitted prunes (about 15)

4¼ ounces (125 grams) dried apricots (about 15)

6 pitted dates

½ teaspoon freshly ground black pepper

8 large eggs, in their shells

1 bay leaf

½ bunch flat-leaf parsley, coarsely chopped

4 large garlic cloves

Preheat the oven to 200°F (93°C).

Make the sauce: Combine the stock, salt, cumin, smoked paprika, sweet paprika, onion powder, garlic powder, red pepper flakes (if using), cinnamon, and black pepper in a large bowl and stir until the sauce is thoroughly combined. Set aside.

Make the adafina: Heat the olive oil in a large Dutch oven over medium heat. When the oil is shimmering, add the onion and cook, stirring frequently, until the onion is translucent and somewhat softened, about 5 minutes. Remove the pot from the heat and set aside.

Cut three 12-inch (30-centimeter) cheesecloth squares.

Place the chickpeas with ½ teaspoon of the salt in the center of one cheesecloth square. Gather up the corners to make a loose beggar's purse and tie them together in such a way that the purse doesn't come apart but there's some slack inside for the contents to expand. Repeat this process with the beans and then the barley, using ½ teaspoon of the salt for each.

Place half the potatoes, sweet potatoes, prunes, apricots, and dates, the black pepper, and all three cheesecloth purses in the Dutch oven over the onion. Top with the remaining potatoes, sweet potatoes, prunes, apricots, and dates.

Tuck the eggs in the nooks between the vegetables and fruits, then scatter the bay leaf, parsley, and garlic over everything.

Pour the sauce over the ingredients in the Dutch oven. Cover the pot, place it in the oven, and cook for at least 8 hours and up to 12 hours. Adafina is usually made overnight, so you should wake up to a delicious smell of food in the morning. Unwrap the purses before serving.

Serve family-style, so everyone can help themselves to vegetables, legumes, grains, and eggs.

Apples

By Dan Barber

You think Eve had it bad? Let me tell you my side of the story.

She and Adam might have been exiled from the garden, but at least they were given clothes to wear. I was plucked from my home and then blamed for Eve's lack of discipline. It wasn't easy, but I clawed my way to other lands, to every corner of the globe: the untold apple diaspora.

But look, I did OK. From the mountains of Asia to the New World, I laid down roots and made my name known. Wherever my seeds were planted, they adapted to and eventually flourished in their new environment. Isn't that the Jewish way? Work hard, move somewhere else, assimilate, and become the best in the trade?

Over time, I became as American as pie. Not bad.

So go ahead, celebrate Rosh Hashanah with apple slices on your table. But while you're dipping them in honey (page 137) to symbolize the sweetness of life, take a moment to consider the struggle behind the sugar.

Some good old-fashioned guilt. What's more Jewish than that?

$\longrightarrow$

APPLE CAKE

Makes one 10-inch (25-centimeter) cake; serves 12

FOR THE FRUIT

2 Fuji apples, peeled, cored, and thinly
sliced

2 Granny Smith apples, peeled, cored, and
thinly sliced

¼ cup (40 grams) dried currants

⅓ cup (65 grams) granulated sugar

1 tablespoon (15 milliliters) fresh lemon
juice

¼ teaspoon ground cardamom

½ teaspoon ground cinnamon

½ teaspoon pure vanilla extract

Pinch of salt

FOR THE CRUMB TOPPING

¼ cup (55 grams) packed light brown
sugar

½ cup plus 2 tablespoons (80 grams)
unbleached all-purpose flour

¼ teaspoon ground cardamom

Pinch of salt

4 tablespoons (½ stick/60 grams)
unsalted butter, cut into ½-inch
(1.5-centimeter) pieces

FOR THE CAKE

8 tablespoons (1 stick/115 grams) unsalted
butter, melted and cooled, plus more
for greasing

2 cups (250 grams) unbleached all-
purpose flour, plus more for dusting

1 teaspoon baking powder

1 teaspoon baking soda

¼ teaspoon salt

3 large eggs, at room temperature

1 cup (220 grams) packed light brown
sugar

1 cup (240 milliliters) sour cream

Confectioners' sugar, for dusting

Position a rack in the center of the oven. Preheat the oven to 350°F (177°C).

Prepare the fruit: Gently toss the apples, currants, sugar, lemon juice, cardamom, cinnamon, vanilla, and salt in a large bowl, until the apples are coated. Set aside.

Make the crumb topping: Combine the brown sugar, flour, cardamom, and salt in a small bowl. Add the butter and, using your fingers, mix in the butter until it is thoroughly incorporated and the mixture resembles small pebbles. (The crumb topping can be made a day in advance, covered, and refrigerated until ready to use.)

Make the cake: Grease a 10-inch (25-centimeter) tube pan with a removable bottom with butter and dust it with flour, tapping out any excess.

In a large bowl, whisk together the flour, baking powder, baking soda, and salt. Set aside.

Whisk together the eggs and brown sugar in a large bowl for about 1 minute, until well combined. Stir in the melted butter, add the sour cream, and mix until combined. Add the flour mixture all at once and use a large rubber spatula to fold it in until completely incorporated. Let the cake batter sit for a couple of minutes to thicken, then fold in the apple mixture and any juices from the bowl.

Transfer the batter to the prepared tube pan and spread it evenly. Sprinkle the crumb topping evenly over the top of the batter. Bake for about 1 hour, until a sharp knife goes easily through the cake and comes out clean.

Place the pan on a wire rack and let the cake cool for about 30 minutes. Run a sharp knife between the cake and the sides of the pan and around the tube to release the cake from the pan. Carefully invert the cake onto another wire rack or a cookie sheet, then place crumb-side up on the wire rack to cool completely. Transfer to a serving plate and dust with confectioners' sugar before serving.

The cake will keep wrapped in plastic wrap in the fridge for 4 to 5 days, or wrapped in a double layer of plastic wrap in the freezer for up to 2 months.

Babka

By David Samuels

My most prized possession during my fractured childhood was a red plastic transistor radio that I religiously kept tuned to 1010 WINS news. "You give us twenty-two minutes, we'll give you the world" was a promise that, minute by minute and hour by hour, helped me maneuver through a landscape of childhood strife. In twenty-two minutes, a war might break out. A three-car accident might close inbound traffic lanes on the Brooklyn Bridge.

When the anxiety became too much for me to handle, I would be packed off to spend the weekend with a Hasidic family in Borough Park or Crown Heights, where parents never fought and children came downstairs freshly washed and dressed for Friday-night dinner. There, I never needed my radio. The families who lived in the solid, modest brick houses were warm and accepting, and they took care of each other. They took me to see their rebbes, each of whom incarnated a different and wondrous style of spiritual kung fu. The Lubavitcher Rebbe's unearthly blue eyes could penetrate your inner soul with a single glance and see everything there was to see there. The Bobover Rebbe was joyous and funny, and his Hasidim were, too. Together, they sang for hours, until their wordless melodies broke open the doors of heaven. The Belzer Rebbe was nice, too.

What these rebbes had in common with me was that we had all, in different ways, been touched by God. Finding a way to express that feeling was the work of a lifetime, which perhaps only a holy

$\longrightarrow$

person could accomplish. But what about the Satmar Rebbe? It was said that Rebbe Yoel was a great *tsadik*, who pursued stringencies that even the Lubavitcher Rebbe, himself a titan, could never have handled, like waiting twenty-four hours to eat dairy after eating meat, perhaps, or fasting for the entire week of Tisha B'Av.

When I got older, I learned that Rebbe Yoel's pursuit of extreme stringencies had led him to board a train to Switzerland at the darkest hour of Jewish history after forbidding members of his community from saving themselves. Better to die, he told them, than to travel to Palestine or America and lose your faith in such godless places. Even today, the story of Rebbe Yoel makes me feel a mixture of fury and helplessness that I associate with being a frightened child, clutching my little radio. There was nothing good about the secrets the Satmar were keeping.

Except I was wrong. When my first son was born, I needed something to serve guests at his bris, and I ventured down to Lee Avenue in Williamsburg, where I discovered the greatest chocolate babka in the world, a tall brioche filled with swirls of moist chocolate lava, which dries on the outside into an impossibly delicious crust. It is available at the Oneg Heimishe Bakery, which goes by other names, and is located just below street level, right across the highway. If you are looking for it, you will find it. And if not, not.

CHOCOLATE BABKA
by Uri Scheft

Makes two 9 by 5-inch (23 by 13-centimeter) babkas

FOR THE DOUGH

½ cup (120 milliliters) whole milk, at room temperature, plus more if needed

½ teaspoon pure vanilla extract

2½ tablespoons (20 grams) fresh yeast, or 2 teaspoons active dry yeast

2¼ cups (280 grams) unbleached all-purpose flour, sifted, plus more if needed and for dusting

2 cups plus 2 tablespoons (220 grams) pastry flour or cake flour, sifted

2 large eggs

⅓ cup (65 grams) sugar

Large pinch of fine sea salt

5 tablespoons plus 1 teaspoon (80 grams) unsalted butter, at room temperature, plus more for greasing

FOR THE FILLING

1½ cups (420 grams) Nutella

1 cup (150 grams) semisweet chocolate chips

FOR THE STREUSEL TOPPING

⅓ cup (65 grams) sugar

1⅔ cups (170 grams) pastry flour or cake flour

8 tablespoons (1 stick/115 grams) cold unsalted butter, cut into very small slivers

FOR THE SIMPLE SYRUP

¾ cup plus 1 tablespoon (160 grams) sugar

½ cup (120 milliliters) water

Make the dough: Put the milk in the bowl of a stand mixer and whisk in the vanilla by hand. Using a fork or your fingers, lightly mix the yeast into the milk. Fit the mixer with the dough hook and add the flours, eggs, sugar, salt, and finally the butter in small pinches.

Set the mixer on the lowest speed and mix, stopping to scrape down the sides and bottom of the bowl as needed and to pull the dough off the hook as it accumulates there and break it apart so it mixes evenly, until the dough is well combined (it will not be smooth), about 2 minutes.

If the dough is very dry, add more milk, 1 tablespoon (15 milliliters) at a time; if the dough looks wet, add more all-purpose flour, 1 tablespoon (8 grams) at a time, until the dough comes together. Increase the mixer speed to medium and mix until the dough is smooth and has good elasticity, about 4 minutes.

Lightly dust your work surface with flour and turn the dough out on top; lightly dust the top of the dough and the interior of a large bowl with flour. Grab the top portion of the dough and stretch it away from you, tearing the dough, then fold it back on top of the dough. Give the dough a quarter turn and repeat the stretch, tear, and fold until you can stretch a small piece of dough very thin without it tearing, about

$\longrightarrow$

5 minutes. Use your hands to push and pull the dough against the work surface in a circular motion to create a nice round of dough. Set the dough in the floured bowl, cover the bowl with plastic wrap, and set aside at room temperature for 30 minutes.

Transfer the dough to a piece of plastic wrap and press it into a 1-inch-thick (2.5-centimeter) rectangle. Wrap the dough in the plastic wrap and refrigerate for at least 1 hour or up to 24 hours.

Lightly grease two 9 by 5-inch (23 by 13-centimeter) loaf pans with butter.

Fill the dough: Unwrap the dough and roll it into a 9 by 24-inch (23 by 60-centimeter) rectangle. Spread the Nutella in an even layer over the dough, all the way to the edges, then sprinkle the chocolate chips in an even layer over the Nutella, across the entire surface of the dough. Working from the top edge, roll the dough into a tight cylinder. As you roll it, push and pull the cylinder a little to make it even tighter. Holding the cylinder by the ends, lift and stretch it slightly to make it even tighter and longer.

Slice the dough in half lengthwise, and set the halves with the exposed layers facing up. Divide the strips in half crosswise to make 4 shorter strips. Overlap one strip on top of another to make an X, making sure the exposed chocolate part of the dough faces up; then twist the ends together like the threads on a screw so you have at least two twists on each side of the X. Place the shaped babka in one of the prepared pans, exposed chocolate–side up. The dough should fill the pan by two-thirds and fit the length perfectly. Cover the pan with plastic wrap. Repeat to shape and twist the remaining 2 pieces of dough, place them in the second prepared pan, and cover with plastic wrap.

Set the loaf pans aside in a warm, draft-free spot until the dough rises 1 to 2 inches above the rim of the pans and is very soft and jiggly to the touch, 2 to 3 hours, depending on how warm your room is (see Note).

Meanwhile, make the streusel: Combine the sugar and pastry flour in a medium bowl. Add the cold butter and use your fingers or a dough cutter to work the butter into the dry ingredients until the mixture looks pebbly and all the butter bits have been incorporated. Cover the bowl with plastic wrap and refrigerate.

Bake the babkas: Preheat the oven to 350°F (177°C). (If you are letting the dough rise in the oven, as described in the Note, be sure to remove the loaf pans and bowl of water before preheating.)

Sprinkle the streusel evenly over the top of both babkas. Bake until the babkas are dark brown and cooked through, about 40 minutes; check them after 25 minutes, and if they are getting too dark, tent them loosely with a piece of parchment paper or aluminum foil.

Meanwhile, make the simple syrup: Combine the sugar and water in a small saucepan and bring to a boil over high heat. Reduce the heat to medium-low and simmer, stirring occasionally, until the sugar has dissolved. Turn off the heat and set the syrup aside to cool.

Remove the babkas from the oven and, while they are still hot, brush the surface of each generously with the cooled sugar syrup, taking care not to brush off the streusel (the syrup makes the top of the babkas shiny and beautiful and also locks in moisture so the cake doesn't dry out; you may not need to use all the syrup— save any extra in an airtight container in the refrigerator and use it for sweetening iced coffee or tea). Run a paring knife between the babkas and the pan edges and turn them out of the pans. Slice and serve warm, or let cool completely in the pans before unmolding and slicing.

NOTE: If your room is very cold, you can speed up the rising process: Set a large bowl of hot water on the floor of the oven, place the loaf pans on the middle oven rack, close the oven door, and let the dough rise. Just remember that your babkas are in there before preheating the oven!

Bagels

By Liel Leibovitz

Are you sitting down? Because I have news for you that you might not want to hear: The bagel is the least Jewish food in the world. Sure, the word itself comes from Yiddish. Right, it was brought to America by Jewish immigrants from Poland. True, it has become synonymous with the American Jewish experience, the archetypal culinary staple of our people. But somewhere along the way, the bagel ascended to the throne of America's most popular breakfast bun, found its way into corners of the country untouched by Jews, and lost its soul. These days, the best bagel joints on earth aren't run by Jews: Absolute Bagels on Manhattan's Upper West Side is owned by Thai immigrants, Montreal's St-Viateur Bagel chain is run by a nice Italian boy, and in Cleveland, two gentiles launched a bagel start-up without ever having stuffed their faces with the doughy delight after fasting on Yom Kippur. Just as foreign to the intricacies of tradition are those members of the tribe who, knowing little about their religion and uninterested in learning, describe themselves playfully as "Bagel Jews," as if some schmear could cover up their discomfort with their heritage. So good-bye, bagel: We may still stack you with lox on a Sunday morning, but you belong to all of America now.

→

IN DEFENSE OF BAGEL JEWS

More than half of American Jews say being Jewish is mainly a matter of ancestry and culture, so I say it's high time we take them at their word and recognize the integrity of Bagel Jews, for whom biting into the perfectly chewy cream cheese–slathered bread of our people is the closest thing there is to a religious experience. In fact, bagels and those who love them are as Jewish as Jewish can be. Jews love a good loophole (did you grow up with Shabbat timers on your lights?), and somewhere between the poor bagel pushcart operators of the Lower East Side and the Lender's Bagel magnates of New Haven, we found our own alternative to eggs Benedict and bacon, egg, and cheese sandwiches in the form of the beloved cream-cheese-and-lox duo.

Of course, as with every Jewish practice, where there are two Jews, there are three opinions about what makes a perfect bagel: toasted or not, boiled or just baked, Brooklyn or Montreal. Still, the fact that the bagel has become a brunch staple gives Jews of all religious bents an opportunity to be as proud of our bread as we are of Leonard Cohen, to claim our place in mainstream culture while honoring our ancestors and preserving our traditions. As for yids in exile (we don't all choose to reside in Brooklyn or Pico-Robertson), there's no action more devout than stocking up on a baker's dozen of our chewy Jewy bread, freezing it, and savoring the limited supply until the next coastal trip.

Danya Shults

HOW TO ASSEMBLE
AN APPETIZING PLATTER

What is a bagel if not for the smoked fish and the schmear? Talmudic scholars have wrestled with this question since biblical times. The answer can be found in an appetizing platter, a choice selection of smoked and cured fish served with bagels, cream cheese (page 94), and other accoutrements on the side.

There's an art to assembling this mainstay of Jewish life, present at celebrations large and small, joyous and somber. You can personalize the platter to your taste, but the classic elements include Nova lox, paprika-rimmed sable, thick-cut kippered salmon, and a whole whitefish. (If you wish to serve pickled herring, place it in a separate bowl off to the side to contain the vinegary juices.) Account for 3 to 4 ounces of fish per guest, depending on their appetites.

Choose a serving platter or board big enough to fit all the fish, then line it with hearty greens, such as kale, lettuce, or collards, that have been thoroughly cleaned and dried. Position the whole whitefish down the center of the platter, peeling back the skin so guests can scoop out the meat. Arrange the other fish around it, each in its own zone. Lay a spoon next to the whitefish, and serving forks or ice tongs near the others. If you plan to replenish the platter while you're entertaining, have preportioned smoked fish ready to go in the fridge.

Place a basket of sliced fresh bagels and toasted bialys (page 36) nearby, as well as bowls of plain and scallion cream cheese (2 ounces per person should do the trick). On another plate, arrange sliced tomatoes and cucumbers, thinly sliced red onion, lemon wedges, and capers.

The irony of assembling such a painstaking spread? It will quickly get demolished.

Bazooka Gum

By Katharine Weber

No other immigrant group is as central to the candy trade as Jews.

One hundred years ago, most confections were generic, sold as penny candy from jars on shop counters or distributed by peddlers, most of them Jewish immigrants from Europe who sold a variety of goods on their rounds. Some of those peddlers arrived in the United States with little more than the clothes they were wearing and an entrepreneurial spirit, and learned the candy trade from their employers. Candy was a relatively easy thing for a newcomer to make. It did not require a significant investment in equipment, materials, or labor, and could be made on a stovetop with a few inexpensive ingredients. Ruined batches were cheap failures, and regular production helped move businesses from home kitchens and pushcarts to retail shops and factories.

Topps was established by the four Shorin brothers in 1938, after their father's American Leaf Tobacco business, founded in 1890 in Crown

Heights, Brooklyn, faltered during the Depression. (Their father, Morris Chigorinsky, changed his name to Shorin after he arrived from Russia in 1888.) Wanting to take advantage of his tobacco distribution channels with a product they could sell to those same outlets, the brothers relaunched the family business with a name—Topps—that echoed the Cole Porter lyric "You're the top!" When sugar was rationed during World War II, Topps bought up small candy companies, closed them, and used their sugar quotas. The company thrived even while larger gum brands went out of business.

Dubble Bubble ruled the bubble gum market when Abraham, Ira, Philip, and Joseph Shorin developed Bazooka bubble gum, recognizing that as World War II ended, the wartime slogan for their spearmint-flavored Topps Chewing Gum, "Don't Talk Chum, Chew Topps Gum!" (a variation of "Loose lips sink ships") was about to become obsolete. Bazooka Joe was modeled after Joseph Shorin, and soon became an iconic American character.

Not bad for a bunch of Jewish brothers from Brooklyn.

GET THE JOKE?

Bazooka gum is, essentially, Jewish Laffy Taffy—except with even more inscrutable jokes.

While the franchise originated in America, along with its profoundly odd "Bazooka Joe" comic strip, its Israeli offshoot and its Hebrew cartoons have become a staple of Jewish life and a favorite of countless candymen in synagogue. There is even an Israeli clothing company for religious women that inexplicably includes a square of the gum in every shipment. And while the American brand discontinued its accompanying comic strip in 2011, the Israeli comic is still going strong, punch line after impenetrable punch line.

Yair Rosenberg

Bialys

By Mimi Sheraton

The bialy was the sole invention and provenance of Jewish bread bakers in Bialystok, Poland. They were much larger in Bialystok than they are in New York—roughly the size of an 8-inch salad plate. I have a photograph taken in 1939 of a boy holding up a bialy, which, by the way, was called a *Bialystoker kuchen*. They were made only in Bialystok. People from the surrounding regions called the Bialystok Jews *Bialystoker kuchen fressers*.

When I was doing research for my 2000 book *The Bialy Eaters*, I got a lot of arguments from people asserting that *bialy* is just a New York name for *pletzel*. But it isn't true. It *is* the same dough, but the form is different. In fact, I developed my own theory as to how the bialy was invented. I think it was indeed made by bakers who made pletzels, which are big onion discs, which in Bialystok always had poppy seeds and, of course, onions. My theory is that a pletzel, having been formed but not baked, fell on the floor and somebody stepped on it with the heel going into the center, then, being frugal, decided to bake it anyway and see what happened. And so the bialy was born.

I interviewed many former Bialystokers about their town's most famous export. They never split them the way we split a bagel. Whatever was going to be put on a bialy, if anything, was put on top. (As Max Ratner, a Bialystok native, told me, "Who could afford to put anything on them?" "Were they a luxury?" I asked. "Darling," he responded, "food was a luxury.")

But what everyone loved most was the fact that the rim was soft while the center was very thin and crisp—which is almost never achieved here in America. Someone in the family always liked the soft part, and someone else liked the crisp part, and it was to the bialy's credit that it could make everyone happy.

$\longrightarrow$

BIALYS

Makes 24 bialys

FOR THE SPONGE

3½ cups (564 grams) bread flour

1 teaspoon active dry yeast

2⅔ cups (631 milliliters) water, at room
temperature

FOR THE FILLING

3 tablespoons (45 milliliters) extra-virgin
olive oil

6 cups (1 kilogram) diced yellow onions
(about 6 medium)

½ teaspoon kosher salt

3 tablespoons (19 grams) poppy seeds

FOR THE DOUGH

3½ cups (564 grams) bread flour, plus
more if needed

½ teaspoon active dry yeast

1 tablespoon kosher salt, plus more for
sprinkling

½ cup (120 milliliters) water, at room
temperature, plus more if needed

Prepare the sponge: Stir together the flour and yeast in a large bowl using a wooden spoon. Make a well in the center and pour in the water. Starting in the center of the well, move the spoon in a circular motion, increasing the area of the well and pulling flour into it until all the flour has been incorporated and you have a homogenous mass, about 3 minutes. The sponge will have a fairly loose consistency.

Cover with plastic wrap and let the sponge sit at room temperature until it doubles in size and develops bubbles on the surface, about 2 hours.

Make the filling: Heat the olive oil in a large skillet over medium heat. Add the onions and salt, reduce the heat to medium-low, and cook, stirring occasionally, until the onions are very soft, golden brown, and substantially reduced in volume, 25 to 30 minutes. Let cool, then stir in the poppy seeds. Set aside.

Make the dough: In the bowl of a stand mixer fitted with the dough hook, mix the flour, yeast, and salt on low speed for 1 to 2 minutes, until combined. Add the water and the sponge and mix on low speed for about 3 minutes to incorporate. Increase the speed to medium and mix for 5 to 7 minutes, until the dough is smooth and starts to pull away from the sides of the bowl. The dough should be shiny, elastic, and somewhat tacky, but not sticky. If the dough is clinging to the sides of the bowl, add more flour 1 tablespoon at a time until it reaches the desired consistency. If the dough feels dry, add more water 1 teaspoon at a time until it reaches the desired consistency.

Line two baking sheets with parchment paper and lightly sprinkle the parchment with flour.

Divide the dough into two equal pieces. Place one piece in a bowl and cover with plastic wrap to prevent it from drying out; set aside.

On a lightly floured work surface, using your hands, flatten the other piece of dough gently until you have released the air bubbles, but do not knead it. (After the dough has risen, it is easier to handle. Kneading it again will make it tight.)

Stretch the dough gently into a rope about 18 inches (46 centimeters) long and, using a bench scraper or a sharp knife, divide it into 12 equal pieces. If you do not have a scale, do your best to estimate the size.

Flatten a piece of dough with the palm of your hand, shaping it into a 3-inch (7.5-centimeter) disk. Gather the sides of the dough into the center and pinch them together, forming a small sphere. Turn the dough over, pinched-side down, and rotate it gently in a clockwise direction, tucking the sides in and making sure it is a completely round, roughly 2-inch (5-centimeter) ball. Place it on a prepared baking sheet and repeat with the remaining pieces of dough. Sprinkle the dough balls lightly with flour, cover with plastic wrap, and let rest for 20 to 30 minutes. Repeat with the second half of the dough.

Line two more baking sheets with parchment paper, or reuse the sheets that the dough is resting on, lining them with fresh parchment paper.

To shape the bialys, place a dough ball on a lightly floured surface, flatten it slightly with your hands, and, using a rolling pin, roll it into a 5-inch (12.5-centimeter) disk. Using your fingers, go around the disk, shaping a ½-inch (1.5-centimeter) rim, then stretch the dough in the center toward the rim until it is thin. Be careful not to tear the dough. Your bialys should have thin, crunchy centers and puffy, soft rims. Press a wide-bottomed glass, about 3 inches (7.5 centimeters) wide, into the center to flatten it. Transfer the disk to a prepared baking sheet and fill it with a scant 2 tablespoons of the filling, spreading it just on the inner part and leaving the rim clean. Sprinkle the filling with a touch of salt. Repeat with the remaining disks, placing them at least 1 inch (2.5 centimeters) apart on the baking sheets.

Put each baking sheet inside a large plastic bag and let the bialys rest for 20 to 30 minutes. Do not let the plastic touch the bialys, as they will puff up a bit.

Position a rack in the center of the oven. Preheat the oven to 500°F.

After the bialys have rested, bake them for 12 to 15 minutes, until golden brown. Let cool on a wire rack.

The bialys will keep in a plastic bag at room temperature for up to 2 days or in the freezer for up to 2 months.

Black-and-White Cookies

By Melissa Clark

Long before Jerry Seinfeld and President Obama declared black-and-white cookies to be an edible symbol of racial harmony, these chocolate-and-vanilla confections were simply a treat my grandmother Ella picked up at our local kosher bakery in Flatbush, along with the mandelbrot and babka. Maybe it was your cousin Rose who got them on the Upper West Side, or your great-uncle Harry in the Bronx. They were all around the city.

Black-and-whites have been an entrenched part of the very robust Jewish cookie scene in New York City for a century. More ubiquitous than rugelach, they are available in bodegas and bagel shops, where they remain as popular as ever.

They didn't necessarily start out as Jewish. Originally from Bavaria, they came to the United States with German immigrants—maybe Jewish, maybe not. Some sources state that the cookies began their American sojourn on the Lower East Side; others point to Utica, New York. Versions of the cookie exist across the Northeast and Midwest, where they go by different names (half-moons, harlequins). The recipe is changeable as well. In some places, they're made from devil's food cake and soft buttercream instead of the lemon-scented sponge cake shellacked with the hardened chocolate and vanilla glazes I knew as a child. Other places use shortbread cookies and fondant.

But wherever or however they're made, their common ground is chocolate and vanilla coexisting on a smooth, sweet surface. They've adapted to their surroundings without losing their essence, just like the Jews (and many other American immigrants, for that matter). And like bagels, Chinese food, and Jerry Seinfeld, they're a deeprooted part of the New York Jewish experience—no matter where you might have experienced them.

$\longrightarrow$

BLACK-AND-WHITE COOKIES

Makes 36 small cookies

FOR THE COOKIES

1¼ cups (160 grams) unbleached all-purpose flour

½ teaspoon baking powder

½ teaspoon salt

1 teaspoon pure vanilla extract

¼ cup (60 milliliters) whole milk

1 teaspoon fresh lemon juice

6 tablespoons (¾ stick/85 grams) unsalted butter, at room temperature

½ cup (170 grams) granulated sugar

1 large egg, at room temperature

FOR THE GLAZES

1½ cups (165 grams) confectioners' sugar

¼ cup plus 1 tablespoon (75 milliliters) whole milk

½ teaspoon pure vanilla extract

¼ cup (25 grams) unsweetened cocoa powder, sifted

Position a rack in the upper third of the oven. Preheat the oven to 375°F (190°C). Line two baking sheets with parchment paper or silicone baking mats.

Sift together the flour, baking powder, and salt into a medium bowl and set aside.

Combine the vanilla, milk, and lemon juice in a small bowl or a measuring cup and set aside.

In the bowl of a stand mixer fitted with the paddle attachment, or in a large bowl using a handheld mixer, beat the butter on high speed for about 1 minute, until light and airy. Gradually mix in the granulated sugar. Add the egg and beat until incorporated, then stop to scrape down the bowl.

With the mixer on medium-low speed, alternately add the flour and milk mixtures in three additions, starting and ending with the flour mixture and mixing until just combined after each addition; stop to scrape down the bowl as necessary.

Use a cookie scoop or a tablespoon to drop 1-tablespoon mounds of dough onto a prepared baking sheet, spacing them about 1½ inches (4 centimeters) apart. Bake in the upper third of the oven for 8 to 10 minutes, until the cookies are firm to the touch and fragrant. Repeat with the remaining batter. Let the cookies cool on the baking sheet for 10 minutes, then transfer them to a wire rack set over a sheet of parchment paper. Turn them over—the flat underside will become the top side of the cookie for easy glazing—then cool completely.

Make the glazes: Combine the confectioners' sugar, ¼ cup (60 milliliters) of the milk, and the vanilla in a small bowl and stir until smooth. Holding a cookie in one hand over the bowl of glaze, use a small spoon to scoop up the glaze and pour it over half the cookie, then, with the back of the spoon, move the glaze around to completely coat half the cookie. Push any excess glaze off the edges so as to fully cover the half. Return the half-glazed cookie to the rack. Repeat with the remaining cookies.

Add the cocoa powder to the glaze remaining in the bowl, then add a teaspoon or two of additional milk, just enough to loosen it—you want it opaque enough to cover the cookie, but thin enough to be workable. Mix until smooth.

Glaze the unglazed half of each cookie as you did with the white glaze. Return them to the rack to set for 30 minutes before eating them or packing them up.

The cookies will keep in an airtight container at room temperature for up to 3 days.

SEPARATE BUT EQUAL?

Now, I love the taste of black-and-white cookies as much as any respectable Jew. But I don't understand why the black-and-white is hailed as a symbol of what a racially harmonious society should look like. It far more accurately illustrates how our society actually functions: Y'know, with black people all on one side, white people all on the other side, and a very thin margin in between where both sides are able to actually meet. How did we get duped into thinking that the baked good representation of the Mason-Dixon Line was something to aspire to?

Brown v. Board of Education didn't happen so we could have "separate but equal" distribution of fondant, people. Let's face it: When Justice Earl Warren said that separation is "inherently unequal," he was talking about the vanilla half of the cookie. Because it's always shittier than the chocolate side.

"See, the key to eating the black-and-white cookie, Elaine," says Jerry on the infamous *Seinfeld* episode that introduced this concept, "is that you want to get some black and some white in each bite. Yet somehow racial harmony eludes us. If people would only look to the cookie, all our problems would be solved!"

Don't do it, people. Don't look to the cookie.

MaNishtana

Blintzes

By Adina Steiman

Blintzes might seem as familiar as other Jewish-food classics like babkas or latkes, but hardly anyone thinks they deserve to be reinvented with a blanket of duck-fat cracklings or a tahini-dosed filling. In fact, now that my grandmother has passed away, I don't know a single person brave enough to attempt them, much less succeed at making them, as she did after decades of practice. But that lack of fashion only proves the blintz's Jewish bona fides. Perhaps it's because, even more than latkes, blintzes require a balaboosta's true mastery of the frying pan.

In fact, "pans" should be plural, since you can't produce blintzes in any useful quantity without having a couple of them going simultaneously—yet another degree of difficulty. But with a master behind the stove, the allure of the blintz, blurred by too many freezer-burned simulacra, comes into sharp focus. Tender and slightly thicker than crepes, the *bletlach* (Yiddish for "leaves") are the foundation of the dish. And just like cooking crepes, cooking bletlach well requires hard-earned muscle memory, since the hot pan engraves every hesitation, every misstep you make with the batter.

Unlike crepes, bletlach are cooked only on one side to maintain a pillowy softness within—a softness that melds with the invariably tender fillings. Cottage cheese (page 92), or farmer cheese, is a classic, but my grandmother never liked the gummy, thickened versions she'd find at the supermarket, so she'd use ricotta cheese, along with a dose of cream cheese for richness and tang. She'd mix in a couple of eggs to help the filling set, and just a tiny bit of vanilla, sugar, and salt to balance the flavor. She wasn't making dessert. She was making *blintzes*. And if her greengrocer had saved her some marked-down, overripe blueberries, they'd go in the bowl, too.

She'd fill and fold dozens of blintzes at a time, regardless of who was coming over, since she knew that they freeze beautifully if separated by sheets of waxed paper. Then, after thawing them for a day in the fridge, she'd give them their final panfrying, browning the tender leaves of those tidy packages until they turned as golden brown as autumn, transforming the sweet dairy within into molten lava ready to be released with the side of a fork. We'd never wait for her to finish frying them to eat them. She insisted we start as soon as they hit the paper towels, and she kept making more as we shouted our praise into the kitchen. Until there were none left.

→

CHEESE BLINTZES

Makes 32 blintzes; serves 6 to 8

FOR THE BLINTZES

4 large eggs

4 tablespoons (½ stick/55 grams) unsalted butter, melted, plus 2 tablespoons (30 grams) at room temperature

1 cup (240 milliliters) whole milk, plus more if needed

1¼ cups (300 milliliters) water, plus more if needed

2 tablespoons (20 grams) sugar

1 teaspoon pure vanilla extract

⅛ teaspoon kosher salt

2 cups (250 grams) unbleached all-purpose flour

FOR THE FILLING

2 cups (455 grams) farmer cheese

1 large egg

½ teaspoon packed lemon zest

3 tablespoons (30 grams) sugar

¾ teaspoon pure vanilla extract

Pinch of kosher salt

Make the blintzes: Place the eggs, 2 tablespoons (29 milliliters) of the melted butter, the milk, water, sugar, vanilla, and salt in the bowl of a food processor. Process for 20 seconds to combine. Add the flour and process for 20 seconds more. Scrape down the sides of the bowl with a spatula, then process for 20 seconds more. The batter will be very smooth and have the consistency of light cream. Transfer the batter to a medium bowl, cover, and refrigerate for at least 1 hour or up to 12 hours.

Stir the batter if it has separated, and add 1 tablespoon (15 milliliters) more water or milk if it has thickened too much. It should have the consistency of heavy cream and flow easily when you tilt the pan to distribute the batter.

Set up your work area: Have a large cutting board, a dish with the remaining 2 tablespoons melted butter, a paper towel folded into quarters, a ladle or ¼-cup (60-milliliter) measuring cup, and a butter knife with a rounded tip near the stove.

Heat a 6-inch (15-centimeter) crepe pan over medium-high heat. Moisten the paper towel with melted butter and use it to grease the pan. Using the ladle or measuring cup, scoop about 3 tablespoons (45 milliliters) of the batter into the skillet and swirl the pan to evenly coat the bottom and partway up the sides. The blintz should be about ¹⁄₁₆ inch (1.5 millimeters) thick, not paper-thin like a crepe.

After about a minute, when the edges of the blintz start to curl, use the tip of the butter knife to gently lift the edge of the blintz to check if it is browning on the bottom—it should be. (If the batter starts to blister and small holes form, reduce the heat slightly.) Cook the blintz on one side only. With one swift motion, flip the pan over the wooden board to release the blintz onto it, browned-side up, leaving enough space on the board for more blintzes to be placed side by side. (Once they have cooled, you can start stacking them on top of one another.) Repeat until all the batter has been used, greasing the pan after making each blintz—the butter prevents them from sticking together when they are stacked.

Make the filling: Place all the filling ingredients in the bowl of a food processor and process for 30 seconds. Scrape the sides of the bowl with a spatula and process again until blended, about 20 seconds more.

Set a blintz in front of you, browned-side up. Place a heaping tablespoon of the filling closer to the upper third of the blintz and flatten it slightly to form a small rectangle, about ½ inch (1.5 centimeters) thick. Lower the upper flap to cover the filling, fold both sides toward the center of the blintz to enclose the filling, and roll the filled portion toward you, ending seam-side down. Repeat until you have used all the filling. (You will have some unfilled blintzes left over. They are delicious folded, fried in butter, and topped with jam.)

To fry the blintzes, melt the remaining 2 tablespoons (30 grams) butter in a nonstick skillet over medium heat. When the butter is sizzling, place a few blintzes in the pan, seam-side down, and cook until golden brown on the bottom, 2 to 3 minutes. Flip them over using two forks and cook until they brown on the second side and puff up, 2 to 3 minutes more.

Serve immediately with sour cream and fresh berries or fruit compote (page 89).

Store filled, unfried blintzes, seam-side down, in an airtight container in the refrigerator for up to 4 days, or stack them between layers of waxed paper and store in an airtight container in the freezer for up to 2 months.

Bokser

(Carob)

By Marjorie Ingall

If you attended a Jewish day school in the twentieth century, chances are, you know from *bokser*. Every Tu B'Shevat, a long, flat, curved, brown carob seed pod showed up on your desk, and you loved it. Despite its being disgusting. Tu B'Shevat celebrates the beginning of spring, and the custom is to eat a new fruit. Bokser was invariably new, always thrilling; it was the only time any of us saw or ate it. We had no idea that bokser was the same substance certain hippie moms tried to foist upon us, telling us it was "as good as chocolate!" It wasn't.

According to the indispensable Jewish etymologist Philologos, the word *bokser* comes from the German *Bockshornbaum*, which means "ram's horn tree." Indeed, the pod resembled a dark, petrified horn. The texture was like that of a dead stick. The smell has been compared to Limburger cheese. The taste, at first, was nonexistent.

Gradually, though, as you sucked and chewed, the slightest hint of chocolate came through. That moment was transcendent.

Alas, your interest and your jaw probably gave out long before you got through the thing; no one has ever finished an entire bokser. (As the goyim say of fruitcake, perhaps there is only a single one that just gets passed around year after year.) But in the years before supermarkets were filled with fruits and veggies from South and Central America, Asia, and Africa, you'd marvel at the fact that this mysterious object in your hand had come all the way from Israel.

Borscht

By Zac Posen

Beets! Their color is like nothing else. I always want to start dyeing fabric in it. I've definitely dipped a napkin or two in my soup to test the colors. (You get a beautiful hot pink.)

When I decided to include a recipe for borscht in my cookbook, *Cooking with Zac*, it raised some eyebrows. It became an experiment in how to make haute borscht. Mine is pureed, and incorporating sour cream creates a more opaque look and adds texture. Something white in your red or pink fuchsia base. I enjoy the combination of the sour bite, the earthy richness of the beet, and the sweetness matched with that incredibly vibrant color from nature. There's something retro and unusual about the flavor of Jewish cuisine because of that sour-sweetness. That's very culturally appropriate. Life brings you sweet moments and sour moments. In Jewishness, as in good borscht, you should be able to find a balance of both.

$\longrightarrow$

BORSCHT

Serves 4 to 6

2 tablespoons (30 milliliters) olive oil

1 medium onion, diced

1 teaspoon kosher salt, plus more to taste

1 bay leaf

2 large garlic cloves, thinly sliced lengthwise

1 large carrot, cut into ⅛-inch-thick (3-millimeter) coins

2 to 3 tablespoons (30 to 45 milliliters) water

2 medium beets, peeled, quartered, and sliced ⅛ inch (6 millimeters) thick

½ teaspoon freshly ground black pepper, plus more to taste

5 cups (1.2 liters) vegetable broth

About ¼ head cabbage, chopped into ½-inch (1.5-centimeter) pieces (2½ cups/170 grams)

1 teaspoon apple cider vinegar, plus more to taste

Sour cream, for serving

Dill sprigs, for garnish

Heat the olive oil in a medium saucepan over medium heat. Add the onion and a pinch of salt and stir to coat with the oil. Add the bay leaf, cover the saucepan, and cook until the onion is translucent, 3 to 4 minutes. Add the garlic, stir to combine, cover, and cook until softened, about 2 minutes.

Add the carrot and a pinch of salt and stir to combine. Reduce the heat to low, cover, and cook, stirring occasionally, until the carrot starts to soften, 7 to 9 minutes—do not let the vegetables brown. Add 1 tablespoon (15 milliliters) of the water if the pan gets too dry.

Add the beets, ½ teaspoon salt, 2 tablespoons (30 milliliters) water, and the pepper to the saucepan and stir to combine. Cook, stirring occasionally, until the beets start to soften, 10 to 15 minutes.

Add the broth, increase the heat to high, and bring the broth to a boil. Add the cabbage, bring to a boil, then reduce the heat to medium-low, cover the pan with the lid ajar, and simmer until the cabbage has softened completely, 20 to 25 minutes.

Add the vinegar. Taste and adjust the seasonings, adding salt, pepper, and/or more vinegar if needed.

Ladle the hot soup into bowls, top with a spoonful of sour cream, and garnish with a sprig of fresh dill.

The soup will keep in an airtight container in the refrigerator for up to 1 week.

THE SECRETS OF SOVIET CUISINE

If you're a North American Jew of a certain vintage whose relatives came from Russia a century ago, Russian staples like borscht, herring (page 135), cabbage rolls (page 252), and rye bread (page 230) are "Jewish food." But as a Soviet-born, Russian-speaking Jew of a more recent vintage, that feels wrong. To me, this food is firmly part of my Soviet-Russian heritage—not my Jewish one.

There's a reason I feel this way.

After seventy years of Communism, Soviet food emerged as a separate branch of Russian (and Ukrainian) food, which developed after the earlier generations of immigrants had already left. What showed up on Soviet Jews' tables was a uniquely historic product of Soviet food policies, broadly applied to all citizens, plus anti-Jewish policies, which successfully erased all religious knowledge from the community. (There were exceptions, but the average Soviet Jew was divorced from any sense of Jewish culinary rules, which explains why pork-laden *sosiski* were an everyday food.)

So what, then, would you find on a Soviet-Jewish table in North America today? The list spans the breadth of the Soviet empire to include countless *zakuski* (appetizers), salads, soups, entrees, and desserts. The familiar herring (for example, *selyodka pod shuba; shuba* means "fur coat," so it's literally "herring under fur coat"), smoked fish, pickles, sprats, our version of *ptcha*, known as *kholodetz*, plus items like Salat Olivier (similar to potato salad, this Tsarist-era invention was adapted into a quintessential Soviet symbol), *kharcho* (a traditional Georgian beef soup, with tomatoes, walnuts, the Georgian spice blend kmehli-suneli, tamarind, and rice), schi (the most Russian of Russian soups, outranking borscht, schi is a cabbage soup, sometimes made with sauerkraut), and *plov*, the national pride of Uzbekistan and Tajikistan, a rice pilaf with lamb, carrots, onions, cumin, and paprika.

Unique among Jewish communities, Soviet Jews didn't separate themselves from their non-Jewish neighbors by their diet—chronic food shortages, communal kitchens, and collectivist idealism hardly encouraged differentiating oneself by dietary preference. As a result, the dishes we brought with us might not always seem so different from broader Soviet cuisine. But these dishes also tell an important part of our story—not just about the way Soviet policies still shape our grocery lists, but of survival and the efforts of our mothers and grandmothers to keep their families alive and fed, whether that was finding *tushenka* (tinned meat) or waiting for hours at the bakery to get a coveted Kiev cake. What makes our food Jewish—and ensures that it will remain so for our children and grandchildren—is that we serve it while openly celebrating Jewish holidays, we make tweaks for kosher observance, and we left the *sosiski* behind along with our Soviet citizenships.

Lea Zeltserman

Brisket

By Amanda Hesser *and* Merrill Stubbs

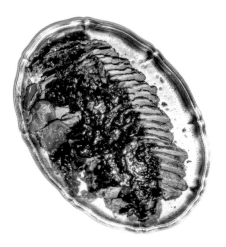

Why are two shiksas writing about brisket for an anthology about iconic Jewish foods? Because we are *jealous.* Jealous that we didn't grow up with brisket—gloriously fatty, juicy, supple brisket. It's the perfect braising beef; brisket is full of flavor, with a thick layer of fat that naturally bastes the meat as it cooks, making it impossible to ruin.

We WASPs were raised on pot roast, a parched cut that seems to beckon inexperienced cooks to boil it dry, and roast beef, which leaves every cook's nerves frayed until the first slice reveals whether you succeeded in coaxing it to just the right pinkness. And you probably didn't. WASPs love their unforgiving meats, just as they relish stony silences at the table.

Jews smartly embraced meats that like to actually be enjoyed. Brisket welcomes acids like vinegar and tomatoes, voraciously absorbs herbs and spices, and gets so tender you needn't own a sharp knife to slice it. And it's great for holidays and parties. You can cook it in advance, lay the slices in a serving dish, soaking in the cooking juices, and reheat it to serve. It'll even be better this way. If you have leftovers, you have the makings of an epic sandwich.

We'll spare you our holiday tables, but can we join yours?

$\longrightarrow$

BRISKET

Serves 8 to 10

3 tablespoons (45 grams) kosher salt

1¼ teaspoons freshly ground black pepper

7 pounds (3 kilograms 175 grams) beef brisket, preferably point (or deckle) cut (see Note)

2 pounds (910 grams) yellow onions, sliced ¼ inch (6 millimeters) thick

1½ pounds (680 grams) carrots (about 5 large), cut ½ inch (1.5 centimeters) thick

1 head garlic (about 10 cloves), cloves peeled

1 (28-ounce/793-gram) can whole peeled tomatoes, drained, juices reserved

½ cup (120 milliliters) apple cider vinegar

¼ cup plus 2 tablespoons (90 milliliters) ketchup

¼ cup (55 grams) dark brown sugar

2 tablespoons (30 milliliters) tomato paste

1 teaspoon garlic powder

1 teaspoon onion powder

¼ cup (60 milliliters) water

2 tablespoons (30 milliliters) blackstrap molasses

2 tablespoons (30 milliliters) pomegranate molasses

Position a rack in the lower third of the oven. Preheat the oven to 350°F (177°C).

Combine 2½ tablespoons (37 grams) of the salt and 1 teaspoon of the pepper in a small bowl. Rub the brisket all over with the salt and pepper.

Scatter half the onions and carrots and all the garlic over the bottom of a large Dutch oven or roasting pan. Place the brisket, point (fat)-side up (see Note), over the vegetables and scatter the remaining vegetables, including the drained tomatoes, on top of the meat.

Combine the reserved tomato juices, the vinegar, ketchup, brown sugar, tomato paste, garlic powder, onion powder, water, and the remaining ½ tablespoon salt and ¼ teaspoon pepper in a medium bowl. Whisk until combined, then pour over the brisket.

Cover the pot with a large piece of parchment paper and place the lid on top, if using a Dutch oven. (If using a roasting pan, omit the parchment paper and cover tightly with heavy-duty aluminum foil.) Transfer to the oven and cook until the meat is very tender, about 3½ hours.

Remove the pot from the oven and trim off any large chunks of fat around the meat. Let come to room temperature, cover, and refrigerate until chilled completely, preferably overnight.

Remove the chilled brisket from the pot and slice it against the grain. Lay the meat in a roasting pan.

Remove about half the onions, half the carrots, and all the tomatoes from the pot and place in the roasting pan with the brisket. Using an immersion blender, puree the braising liquid and the onions and carrots remaining in the pot until smooth. Transfer the liquid to a medium saucepan and add the blackstrap molasses and pomegranate molasses. Bring the liquid to a simmer over medium heat and cook, stirring, until the gravy has thickened, about 7 minutes. Pour half the thickened gravy over the sliced meat and vegetables, and reserve the rest.

To serve the brisket, preheat the oven to 350°F (165°C).

Cover the pan with foil and warm the brisket until heated through, 30 to 45 minutes. Serve hot or warm, with the reserved warmed gravy and the accompanying vegetables.

NOTE: Because the whole brisket contains both the point and the flat parts, it's important to tell your butcher which one you want. The point has more fat on it, so slow cooking it will give you a more tender brisket, because the fat will protect and moisturize the meat.

OVERNIGHT METHOD: To make the brisket overnight, preheat the oven to 200°F (93°C). Cook for 10 to 12 hours following the method above.

SLOW COOKER METHOD: To make the brisket in a slow cooker, follow the steps above, but place everything in a large slow cooker, cover, and cook on Low for 10 to 12 hours.

TO MAKE AHEAD: The brisket can be made ahead and frozen. To freeze, cool the brisket to room temperature, then transfer to a glass container with a tight-fitting lid, cover, and freeze for up to 3 months.

Burnt Offerings
(Sacrifices, Barbecue, Etc.)

By Liel Leibovitz

Aaron Franklin of Austin, Texas, probably the world's greatest barbecue pitmaster, smoked his very first kosher brisket in 2017. He wasn't having a religious awakening; he was honoring Ari White and Izzy Eidelman, two Jews who captured the coveted Brisket King NYC title (the king of "kosher bacon"), in 2016 and 2017 respectively. The sinewy cut, of course, has long been a staple of both Jewish cooking and American barbecue, but the latter's love affair with pork—pulled, ribs, or otherwise—meant that historically, Jews were largely absent around the barbecue pit. Not anymore, and amen to that: If you're looking for the world's first recipe for grilled meat, after all, look no further than Leviticus, which instructs the Israelites on how to build a pit and roast the burnt offering. With the bond between beef and holiness secured early on, and with kashrut paying close attention to slaughtering cattle in a specific way, sanctifying the moment of their sacrifice, it was only a matter of time before Jews returned to the fore of the meat scene.

Carciofi alla Giudia

By Paola Gavin

Carciofi alla giudia—"artichokes Jewish-style"—is probably the most famous dish of Rome's Jewish cuisine. The crispy artichokes, fried in olive oil, were created in the ghetto in the sixteenth century and are traditionally served to break the fast of Yom Kippur, the Day of Atonement. Unfortunately, it is one of those dishes that can taste sublime or like a piece of old leather, depending on the skill and knowledge of the chef and the variety of artichoke used. In Rome, it is always made with *cimaroli*—violet-tinged artichokes that are very tender, with no fuzzy chokes and, most important, leaves without thorns. My advice is, if you cannot get ahold of cimaroli or similar tender artichokes, don't waste your time. Having said that, according to the Talmud, "one may trim the artichoke and *akivrot* [cardoons] on a festival"—so Jews have been enjoying artichokes for millennia, no matter how difficult they are to prepare.

CARCIOFI ALLA GIUDIA

Serves 4 to 6 as an appetizer

3 lemons: 2 cut in half, 1 cut into wedges

2 pounds (10 kilograms) baby artichokes
(about 16)

Olive oil, for frying

Salt

Fill a large bowl with water. Squeeze the 2 halved lemons into the water and add the spent halves to the bowl, too. Set the bowl near your work area.

Clean the artichokes by removing their tough dark outer leaves. When you get to the light-colored interior leaves, trim the stems of whatever tough bits there may be and trim about ½ inch (1.5 centimeters) off the tip. Drop each cleaned artichoke into the prepared lemon water.

Bring a medium pot of water to a boil over high heat. Fill a large bowl with ice and water and set it nearby. Add the artichokes to the boiling water and blanch for 15 seconds, then dunk them into the bowl of ice water and let cool.

Remove the cooled artichokes from the bowl and shake off excess water. Using a paring knife, cut down the middle of each artichoke from the top along the length of the artichoke. When you get through the leaves to the base, stop. Rotate the artichoke and make a similar cut perpendicular to the first cut, making an X. You should now have four quadrants of leaves.

Pry the leaves open, creating a flower-like shape. Place the artichokes stem-side up on a paper towel–lined work surface or baking sheet to keep the leaves open. Allow to dry for at least 20 minutes or up to 2 hours.

When ready to cook, heat 2 inches (5 centimeters) of olive oil in a medium pot over medium-high heat to 350°F (177°C). Using tongs, place an artichoke in the hot oil, stem-side up, holding it against the bottom of the pot for several seconds to fry the leaves open in place. Release the artichoke, then repeat with 4 to 5 additional artichokes, taking care not to overcrowd the pot. Fry the artichokes for about 2 minutes more, moving them around in the pot and rotating them onto their sides to cook evenly. Transfer the fried artichokes to a paper towel–lined baking sheet and season with salt. Repeat to fry the remaining artichokes.

Serve with the lemon wedges alongside.

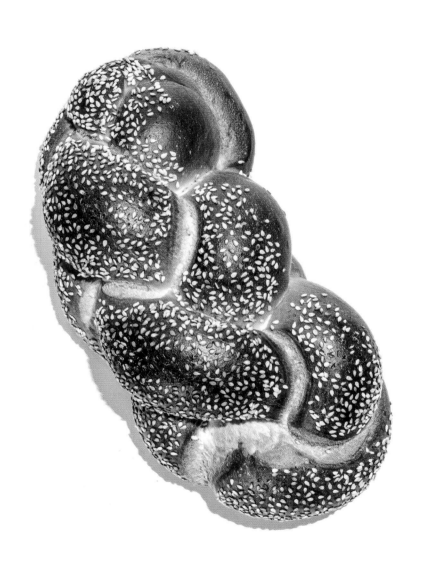

Challah and Other Sabbath Breads

By Leah Koenig

The Sabbath dinner table carries a hefty symbolic weight on top of its four legs and freshly pressed tablecloth. After the destruction of the Holy Temple in Jerusalem, the rabbis transferred many of the rites once performed there—lighting candles, blessing wine, washing hands—to the home table. At the center of this domestic altar is bread: loaves meant to represent the "showbread" that was once placed on the altar as a divine offering. So each Friday night, as people lift and bless their bread before tucking into the festive meal, they are—knowingly or not—reenacting an ancient priestly ritual.

Traditionally, Sabbath tables are graced with at least two loaves of bread (*lechem mishneh*), which symbolizes the double portion of manna the Israelites gathered before the Sabbath while wandering in the wilderness. Today, lechem mishneh most widely refers to challah—eggy loaves that are wound into thick braids and baked until tender and bronzed. Challah's twisted shape dates back to fifteenth-century Austria and southern Germany. Before then, Sabbath bread was typically made from fine white flour but did not have a specific shape or name. It is there, Gil Marks writes in the *Encyclopedia of Jewish Food*, that Jews adopted the shape of a Teutonic solstice bread, braided to resemble the "long, matted hair" of a malevolent demon called Berchta or Frau Holle. "Although

→

European Jews certainly did not worship or even to a large extent know anything about [her], they assimilated the attractive bread," Marks writes. That Jews bless a bread originally modeled after a pagan witch is irony at its most delicious.

Challah is closely related to *berches* (also called water challah), a braided loaf enriched with mashed potato instead of eggs, which German Jews bless on Shabbat. In other parts of the world, Sabbath bread takes on other forms. Ethiopian Jews prefer *dabo*, a soft, honey-sweetened loaf spiced with turmeric and nigella. Tunisian Jews, meanwhile, eat *bejma*, a yeasted bread formed into doughy triangles, and Moroccan and Syrian Jews traditionally decorate their Sabbath tables with whole wheat flatbreads called *khubz 'adi*.

Egg challah has transcended the Sabbath table and also the Jewish community. Its plush texture makes it the ideal bread for French toast, a quality that delis and diners across America have capitalized on. But at its core, it's a bread with serious soul.

CHALLAH
by Einat Admony

Makes 4 loaves

2½ cups (600 milliliters) whole milk or water

8⅔ cups (1.16 kilograms) unbleached all-purpose flour, plus more for dusting

1½ tablespoons (12 grams) active dry yeast

¾ cup (180 milliliters) honey or (150 grams) sugar

¼ cup (60 milliliters) canola oil, plus more for the bowl

3 large eggs

1½ tablespoons (23 grams) kosher salt

White sesame or nigella seeds, for sprinkling

Heat the milk in a small saucepan over low heat until it's just warm to the touch.

Dump the flour into a large bowl and make a well in the center. Add the yeast to the well along with a few drops of the honey and ½ cup (120 milliliters) or so of the warm milk. Let stand until foamy, about 10 minutes.

In a separate bowl, combine the remaining milk and honey, the canola oil, and 2 of the eggs. Stir together. Add the salt and stir again. Gradually stir the liquid mixture into the flour, about ½ cup (120 milliliters) at a time. When the dough becomes sticky and difficult to stir, dump it onto a floured surface and knead it by hand, adding a little more flour if necessary to keep it from sticking, until smooth and elastic.

Knead the dough into a ball. Grease a large bowl with oil, add the dough, and turn the dough to coat with oil. Cover with a damp cloth and let stand in a warm place until the dough has doubled in size, 1 to 1½ hours.

Line two baking sheets with parchment paper.

Gently punch the dough down and turn it out onto a floured surface. Divide the dough into four equal portions, working with one portion at a time and keeping the rest covered with a damp cloth. Divide one portion of dough into 3 equal pieces and roll into ropes about 12 inches (30 centimeters) long and slightly tapered.

Line the ropes up on a baking sheet and braid, pinching the ends to seal and tucking them underneath. Repeat with the remaining dough to make 4 braided loaves. Cover with a damp cloth and let stand until nearly doubled in size, 25 minutes or so.

Preheat the oven to 350°F (177°C).

Lightly beat the remaining egg and brush it over the loaves. Sprinkle with seeds. Bake until golden brown, 20 to 30 minutes.

Charoset

By MaNishtana

Passover is the most celebrated Jewish holiday in the world, reaching across the ever-widening denominational aisles to unite Jews in a shared sense of culture and history. For African American Jews, Passover feels ever more real, tangible. For us, the Seder plate isn't something symbolic of an event that happened to "ancestors" a long, long time ago in a country far, far away. It's about experiences that happened to family—our grandparents, great-grandparents, great-great grandparents—of whom we have photographs and maybe even had the privilege of actually knowing, in the country we actually live in.

When it comes to culture and history, no food merges the two as deftly as the chunky concoction known as charoset—representing the mortar from which the Jews formed their bricks in Egypt. Gibraltarian recipes use real ground bricks, and Persian ones include forty different ingredients for each year the Jews spent in the desert, while the charoset of African American Jews consists of the slave crops of pecans, cocoa powder, figs, and sugarcane. No matter what recipe you use, charoset pays homage to our ancestral story of slavery while representing a unique expression of Jewish Diasporic experiences anywhere across the globe.

$\longrightarrow$

CHAROSET

Serves 6 to 8

3 large, crisp apples such as Gala, McIntosh, or Fuji, peeled, cored, and diced

10 dried figs, coarsely chopped (about 1 cup/177 grams)

¼ cup (60 milliliters) honey

Zest of 1 lemon

1 tablespoon (15 milliliters) fresh lemon juice

1½ teaspoons ground cinnamon

⅔ cup (160 milliliters) sweet red wine, such as Manischewitz

1 cup (100 grams) walnuts, toasted, cooled, and coarsely chopped

Place two-thirds of the diced apples in a large skillet. Add the figs, honey, lemon zest, lemon juice, cinnamon, and wine. Bring to a simmer over medium heat and cook, stirring occasionally, until the apples and figs have softened and absorbed the wine, 7 to 10 minutes. Remove from the heat and let cool for a few minutes, until the mixture is no longer boiling hot.

Place the cooked fruit in the bowl of a food processor. Add the walnuts and pulse until the mixture is thick and fairly smooth—it's OK if there are still some crunchy walnut bits. Transfer the mixture to a large bowl and fold in the remaining raw apples.

To serve the charoset in the shape of a pyramid, mound it into the center of a large plate or serving platter. Working from the top, use an offset spatula or butter knife to sculpt the charoset into four triangular sides with a square base that meet at a point at the top. Work until each side is smooth and equal in size. Decorate if desired.

GOING GLOBAL

Unlike many Jewish foods, which unintentionally resemble stuff hefty enough to spackle together pyramids, this quality is charoset's raison d'être. It's mortar by design, a sweet and spiced mishmash of fruit, nuts, and wine that plays an essential role in the Passover Seder.

While the Ashkenazi mélange of apples (page 19), wine (page 278), walnuts, and cinnamon might be most familiar to Americans, there's more than one way to make paste. For Sephardim and Mizrahim, dates (page 96) are the foundation of charoset. In Georgia, you'll likely detect pears. In Curaçao, peanuts and cashews may be in play. The recipes vary from culture to culture, country to country, and interpretation to interpretation.

While charoset is a stand-in for mortar, it's not all about mud. The ingredients themselves are symbolic. The inclusion of fruit and acid, for instance, alludes to a verse in the Song of Songs that mentions *tapuach*, a disputed fruit (the translation could be quince or *etrog*, but the word means "apple" in Hebrew) that has come to denote hope in times of despair. The addition of long spices, meanwhile, such as cinnamon or ginger, symbolizes the straw used by Jewish slaves in Egypt to make bricks.

The opportunities for riffing are vast. Some cultures use dried fruit, such as dates, figs, apricots, and raisins, to form the body of their charoset. Others mix fresh and dried fruit together. The types of nuts, wine, spices, and sweeteners are also subject to change. One recipe for Afghan charoset lists sixteen ingredients, including bananas, strawberries, and black pepper. In Italy, chestnuts are a common addition. A Persian charoset brings cardamom into the mix, along with coriander, cloves, and cinnamon. A recipe from Surinam features seven dried fruits, including coconut, plus cherry jam.

The flavor profile is consistently sweet, and the possibilities are endless.

Cheesecake

By Daphne Merkin

This silky-smooth baked confection, creaminess masquerading as a cake, sets my salivary glands dripping. Best served on Shabbos morning as padding for the several hours of shul-going ahead, or at a Shavuot dinner, cheesecake is a shout-out to the magnificence of all things light and sweet: cream cheese (page 93), eggs, sugar. For people raised on Jewish cuisine, the unalloyed *milchigness* of cheesecake comes as something of a relief, a counterpoint to the dominant melody of cholent and brisket. If it isn't a quintessentially Jewish dessert, it should be legislated as one—proof that sometimes simplicity wins out, even for a people who have God on the brain.

CHEESECAKE WITH CHERRIES

Makes one 9-inch (23-centimeter) cheesecake; serves 12

FOR THE CRUST

4 tablespoons (½ stick/60 grams) unsalted butter, melted, plus more for greasing

1¾ cups (215 grams) graham cracker crumbs (from 14 graham crackers)

¼ cup (50 grams) sugar

1 teaspoon kosher salt

FOR THE CHEESECAKE

3½ (8-ounce/225-gram) packages cream cheese, at room temperature

1¼ cups (250 grams) sugar

¾ teaspoon kosher salt

2 teaspoons pure vanilla extract

4 large eggs, at room temperature

1¼ cups (300 milliliters) sour cream

Finely grated zest of 1 lemon

Boiling water, as needed

FOR THE CHERRY TOPPING

1 (10-ounce/284-gram) package frozen pitted sour cherries or sweet cherries

½ cup (100 grams) sugar (if using sweet cherries, reduce to ¼ cup/50 grams)

2 tablespoons (30 milliliters) fresh lemon juice

1 tablespoon (8 grams) cornstarch

3 tablespoons (45 milliliters) water

Make the crust: Position a rack in the center of the oven. Preheat the oven to 350°F (177°C). Grease a 9-inch (23-centimeter) springform pan with butter. Wrap the bottom of the pan with enough aluminum foil to protect the cake from the water bath.

Stir together the graham cracker crumbs, sugar, and salt in a large bowl until combined. Pour in the melted butter and stir until all the dry ingredients are uniformly moist and the mixture resembles wet sand. Transfer the mixture to the prepared pan and, using your fingers, pat it into an even layer over the bottom of the pan.

Place the pan on a baking sheet and bake until the crust is lightly brown, about 10 minutes. Transfer the springform pan to a wire rack. Reduce the oven temperature to 325°F (163°C).

Make the cheesecake: In the bowl of the stand mixer fitted with the paddle attachment, beat the cream cheese on medium speed for about 4 minutes, until soft and creamy. With the mixer running, add the sugar and salt and beat for 4 minutes more, until the cheese is light. Beat in the vanilla, then add the eggs one at a time, beating for 1 minute after each addition. Reduce the mixer speed to low and add the sour cream and lemon zest. Beat until combined.

Place the springform pan in a roasting pan large enough to hold the pan with some space around it. Give the cheesecake batter a few stirs to make sure that the

→

bottom doesn't have any unmixed bits, then scrape the batter into the springform pan over the crust. The batter should reach the rim of the pan. Place the roasting pan in the oven and pour enough boiling water into the roasting pan to come halfway up the sides of the springform pan.

Bake the cheesecake for 1½ hours, until the top is brown and maybe cracked. Turn off the oven and open the oven door just a smidge (you can keep it ajar with the handle of a wooden spoon). Let the cheesecake sit in the oven for 1 hour more.

Carefully pull the roasting pan out of the oven and lift the springform pan out and onto a rack. Carefully remove the foil from around the springform pan. Let the cheesecake cool in the pan.

When the cake is cool, cover the top loosely and refrigerate for at least 4 hours and up to overnight (overnight is better, as it allows the flavors to settle).

Make the topping: Combine the cherries, sugar, lemon juice, cornstarch, and water in a medium saucepan. Bring to a simmer over medium heat, reduce the heat to low, and cook, stirring frequently, until the cherries are soft and the sauce has thickened, 8 to 10 minutes. Remove from the heat, transfer to a jar, cover, and let cool completely before serving.

When ready to serve, unmold the cheesecake by carefully unclasping the sides of the springform pan. If the cheesecake is sticking to the sides, run an offset spatula between the pan and the cheesecake to loosen it. Transfer the cheesecake to a serving platter, top with the cherries, and serve immediately.

WHY JEWS EAT CHEESECAKE ON SHAVUOT

As you probably know, it's traditional to eat dairy foods on Shavuot. What's less clear is why. Because the holiday is simultaneously a harvest festival and a commemoration of the Israelites receiving the Torah at Mount Sinai, the first and most obvious guess is that we're celebrating "a land flowing with milk and honey" (Exodus 3:8). Some lesser-known theories include a kabbalistic one, noting that the Hebrew word *halav* (milk) has a numerological value of 40 (*het* = 8, *lamed* = 30, *vet* = 2), which is also the same number of days Moses spent on Mount Sinai before returning with the Ten Commandments (did I just blow your mind?). Another wordplay-oriented theory—the Jews love wordplay—notes that Mount Sinai is called Gavunim ("multiple peaks") in the Book of Psalms (68:15), and *gavunim* shares a root with, or at least the same Hebrew letters as, *g'vinah*, which means "cheese." Of course it does.

Marjorie Ingall

Chicken. Just Chicken.

By Wayne Hoffman

"Jews and chicken," said Grace Adler on the 2006 finale of the now resurrected *Will & Grace*. "It's deep, and it's real."

There's no debating that Jewish cuisine would wither without chicken. No chicken means no schmaltz (page 236), which means half the delicious things your grandmother used to make suddenly become half as delicious. No chicken means Shabbat dinners with a giant empty spot on your plate, a hole that no meat loaf or risotto or tofu scramble can fill. No chicken means matzo ball soup with *kneidlach* floating in—what? Beef bouillon? Hearty vegetable? Mushroom barley? Hot water? Come on.

$$\longrightarrow$$

But what explains Jews' connection to chicken, as opposed to, say, beef or lamb? Simple. As anyone who's ever eaten both kosher and nonkosher meat can attest, kosher red meat is second-rate. (Yes, yes, I'm sure your butcher is a magician, and your preparation is perfection, and your roast is top-notch. But please. Try *treyf* beef, just once. Seriously.) Kosher substitutes for pork products like bacon and sausage are best left undiscussed—and uneaten. As for fish, what's kosher is perfectly lovely, but leaving shellfish off the menu altogether is like listening to a symphony without the woodwinds; what's there may sound wonderful, but everyone can tell something's missing.

Chicken, on the other hand, is the one place where the Jews got it right in the flavor department. Kosher chicken is so vastly superior to any *treyf* bird—bigger, juicier, more flavorful—that they're barely birds of a feather. Perdue's legendary Oven Stuffer roasters look like sparrows next to an average kosher chicken; Tyson's scrawny and pale (so pale!) birdlets can't compete, either. Have you ever seen a *treyf* drumstick? More like a matchstick.

So of course Jews love chicken. It's the only place on a kosher menu where they don't have to settle for second best.

ROAST CHICKEN STUFFED WITH LEMON AND HERBS

by Joan Nathan

Serves 4 to 6

1 (4- to 5-pound/1.8- to 2.25-kilogram) chicken

5 garlic cloves: 4 left whole, 1 cut in half

4 tablespoons (60 milliliters) olive oil

Kosher salt and freshly ground black pepper

2 lemons

2 sprigs rosemary

2 sprigs thyme

2 sprigs sage

2 medium yellow onions, quartered

2 celery stalks, cut into 1-inch (2.5-centimeter) pieces

2 medium carrots, cut into 1-inch (2.5-centimeter) pieces

3 medium beets, quartered

1 medium fennel bulb, quartered

1 medium celery root, cut into 1-inch (2.5-centimeter) pieces

1 pound (455 grams) potatoes, cut into 1-inch (2.5-centimeter) pieces

1 cup (240 milliliters) dry white wine

2 tablespoons (6 grams) chopped fresh parsley, for garnish

Rinse and thoroughly dry the chicken. (A wet chicken will steam rather than roast, so be diligent.) Put the chicken in a large roasting pan. Rub the skin with the cut sides of the halved garlic clove (reserve the garlic clove).

Brush 2 tablespoons of the olive oil over the chicken and sprinkle generously with salt and pepper. Halve one of the lemons and insert it into the cavity of the chicken, followed by the reserved halved garlic clove, the rosemary, thyme, and sage.

Scatter the remaining 4 garlic cloves, the onions, celery, carrots, beets, fennel, celery root, and potatoes around the chicken, nestling them together if necessary. Thinly slice the remaining lemon and scatter it on top. Drizzle with the remaining 2 tablespoons (30 milliliters) olive oil and sprinkle with more salt and pepper. Pour the wine over the vegetables.

Put the pan in a cold oven. Turn on the oven to 375°F (190°C) and roast the chicken, basting it occasionally with the pan juices, until golden and cooked through, 1½ to 2 hours.

Remove the lemon from the cavity and let the chicken rest for about 10 minutes.

In the meantime, spoon the vegetables onto a serving platter, leaving space in the middle for the chicken. Chop up the lemon from the cavity and scatter it over the vegetables, along with the parsley. Set the chicken in the center and serve.

Chicken Soup

By Joan Nathan

Let's start with a hard truth: Chicken soup actually predates Judaism. It was, in fact, the Chinese who brought the chicken and its soup to the West. Ever since chickens were domesticated—between seven thousand and ten thousand years ago—the bird, bathed in water in a clay pot with a few vegetables to form a soup, has been a special dish in China.

But our own history with the dish begins illustriously and keeps on going. In the twelfth century, the great doctor and philosopher Maimonides learned from Chinese and Greek texts about chicken soup's medicinal qualities. Indeed, the idea of chicken soup as the "Jewish penicillin" derives from his treatise *On the Causes of Symptoms*, in which he recommends "chicken soup be used as a cure for whatever might ail you." Maimonides also prescribed a soup or stew made with an old hen or cock as a panacea for the common cold and other ailments.

The flavors of this once simple soup, made with water, chicken, onions, carrots, celery, dill (page 101), parsley, and an occasional parsnip, have evolved with the times. Years ago, when I lived in Israel, I tasted Yemenite chicken soup with garlic, cumin, coriander, fenugreek, and Persian *abgoosht* seasoning, which is flavored with cardamom and turmeric. And with the increase of immigration to the United States, we are discovering tasty recipes from the great Jewish Diaspora and beyond, introducing unexpected flavors and continually transforming this perennial comfort food. Over the years, we have treated our taste buds to Azerbaijani, Uzbek, and Colombian Jewish chicken soups laced with cumin, turmeric, ginger, and other ancient yet modern healing spices. And today, when I'm sick, I long for another alternative—Vietnamese pho with chicken.

Still, it's hard to separate oneself from the classic, and the role it has played in our lives, individually and communally—and anyway, who would want to?

JEWISH PENICILLIN: FACT OR MYTH?

In an experiment in 2000, a scientist at the University of Nebraska Medical Center proved what your mother has been saying for years: Chicken soup cures the common cold. The study, performed by Dr. Stephen Rennard, found that chicken soup inhibits neutrophil chemotaxis in vitro. (In plain English: "We found chicken soup might have some anti-inflammatory value" and "may ease the symptoms of upper respiratory tract infections.")

→

CHICKEN SOUP

Serves 6

1 (4-pound/1.8-kilogram) chicken, cut into 8 pieces, backbone reserved

2 large yellow onions, unpeeled, quartered

3 celery stalks, coarsely chopped

1 small head garlic, halved through the equator

Handful of flat-leaf parsley sprigs, plus more for serving

Handful of dill sprigs

1 tablespoon (15 grams) whole white or black peppercorns

1 tablespoon (15 grams) kosher salt, plus more as needed

10 medium carrots (1½ pounds/ 680 grams), cut into 2-inch (5-centimeter) pieces

1 large parsnip (½ pound/227 grams), peeled and cut into 2-inch (5-centimeter) pieces

3½ quarts (3.5 liters) water

Combine the chicken pieces and backbone, onions, celery, garlic, parsley, dill, peppercorns, and salt in a large pot. Add half the carrots and the parsnip to the pot and cover with the water. Bring to a boil, then reduce the heat so the liquid is at a simmer. Cook, skimming off and discarding any gray scum that rises to the top, until the chicken breasts are cooked through and firm to the touch, 20 to 25 minutes. Transfer the chicken breasts to a bowl and cover so they don't dry out, then cook the stock for about 3 hours more, stirring it here and there (once an hour or so). Be sure to skim any gray scum that floats to the top. At this point, the stock should be a rich yellow-gold color and the remaining chicken pieces and vegetables should be mushy and spent.

Strain the stock through a cheesecloth-lined sieve into a large bowl and return it to the pot. Discard the solids in the sieve. Bring the stock back to a lively simmer over medium-high heat and add salt to taste.

While the stock is simmering, discard the chicken breast skin and bones and shred the meat. Set aside.

Add the remaining carrots to the soup, reduce the heat to low, and cook at a gentle simmer until the carrots are tender, about 15 minutes. Add the shredded chicken breast meat to the soup and let it warm up, 2 to 3 minutes. Ladle the soup into bowls and top each with some parsley. Serve immediately.

Chinese Food

By Action Bronson

In New York City, Chinese food is as Jewish as matzo ball soup. For Jews, eating Chinese food is like getting taken to the Taj Mahal, for real—it's a big deal. Every New York Jew loves Chinese food. They can be Jewish, but they'll still eat that Chinese rib. They'll still eat that roast pork. They'll still eat that fried rice. Lo mein is heavy-duty in the Jewish community.

One of the biggest staples in my Jewish household was the egg foo young my mother would purchase. I don't fuck with it, but my mother would always get it with that sauce—that's old-school shit. For years, I would get chicken and broccoli, until I started getting sesame chicken, and then General Tso's or kung pao. But always with an egg roll—and always hot mustard. There were so many little cups of that mustard in my house, I never even had to ask for them. There were times when I had Chinese food six times a week. I had Chinese food yesterday: I had kung pao chicken, beef with rice noodles, and Szechuan cucumbers.

Chinese food is not a phase. This is forever, this is a lifestyle—a Jewish lifestyle.

→

WHY JEWS EAT CHINESE FOOD ON CHRISTMAS

The Hebrew year is 5779 and the Chinese year is 4717. That must mean, the joke goes, that against all odds, the Jews went without Chinese food for 1,062 years. In fact, Jewish love for Chinese food is neither hallucinated nor arbitrary. It is very real and very determined, and it originated roughly a century ago, on the Lower East Side of Manhattan.

The predominant groups in the area were Eastern European Jews, Italians, and Chinese. According to Matthew Goodman, author of *Jewish Food: The World at Table*, Italian cuisine and especially Italian restaurants, with their Christian iconography, held little appeal for Jews. But the Chinese restaurants had no Virgin Marys. And they prepared their food in the Cantonese culinary style, which utilized a sweet-and-sour flavor profile, overcooked vegetables, and heaps of garlic and onions. Sound familiar?

Additionally, argued Gaye Tuchman and Harry G. Levine in a 1992 academic paper titled "Safe Treyf," Chinese food featured the sort of unkosher dishes you could take home to your mother, or at least eat in front of her. For one thing, there is no mixing of dairy and meat, for the simple reason that there is no dairy. (Think about it!) Of course, there is *treyf* aplenty, chiefly pork and shellfish. But it is always either chopped and minced and served in the middle of innocuous vegetables all covered in a common sauce, or wrapped up in wontons and egg rolls—where you can't see it. Goodman notes that the proprietors of Chinese restaurants eventually picked up on this: "They would advertise wonton soup as chicken soup with *kreplach*."

The final part of this story is the one you already know: Most Chinese people are not Christian. Therefore, on Christmas, Chinese restaurants are open.

OK, you say, but since the Lower East Side's glory years, and even since the baby boomers' halcyon suburbia, many more options have cropped up—Indian, Korean, Thai. But still, as Rabbi Joshua Plaut, author of *A Kosher Christmas*, says, "For Jews, the decision to go to a Chinese restaurant on Christmas is conscious and intended."

"It's a love affair and a sacred tradition to partake of Peking duck," Plaut quips. He argues that to eat Chinese on Christmas is a ritual, not unlike the rituals that traditional Judaism—which has always valued observance where Christianity has valued faith—requires. For some, the Chinese-on-Christmas experience is a replacement for traditional rituals: a prayer you can eat.

Marc Tracy

Cholent

By Shalom Auslander

People talk to me about cholent.

I don't know why, but they do.

At parties, at book festivals, at coffee shops.

They really shouldn't.

"You should come over!" they say. "I'll make cholent!"

It's like running into Oliver Twist forty years after he left the work-house and inviting him over for a nice bowl of gruel. I hate cholent. I hate the sound of the word, I hate even typing it, and I'm going to have to shower as soon as I'm done writing this. It reminds me of everything I hate about my history. It's a steaming-hot bowl of childhood, and just for the record, I'm severely cholent-intolerant.

"C'mon, Oliver! Gruel! You remember gruel!"

Assholes.

It's not cholent's fault. What's to hate, after all? A stew made of beans, meat, potatoes, and bones—it's delicious. But the whole is more grating than the sum of its parts. Ostensibly, it was a way around the prohibition of cooking on Shabbos (the only thing rab-bis love more than cholent is a good loophole), but my mother was unable to bring the bowl out to the table without reminding us that Jews were poor and miserable—"They were peasants!"—and so the

$\longrightarrow$

poor and miserable Jews had nothing to eat but this poor and miserable peasant stew, no doubt while fleeing Somewhere for Somewhere Else, from which they would soon flee again. The smell alone is enough to make me depressed.

"My mother made it with chickpeas!" people tell me.

Really? Mine made it with guilt and bile.

I prefer the jelly doughnuts on Hanukkah. They're white and bright and sweet and sugary; in hindsight, I'm surprised I wasn't taught that the jelly represents the blood of my poor and miserable ancestors, the powdered sugar their tears. When I die and no doubt go to hell (you will, too, trust me; we all do), God will meet me at the gates with a steaming bowl of that loathsome too-Jew stew in His hands, an evil grin on His old bastard face.

"C'mon, Shalom! Cholent! You remember cholent!"

Asshole.

CHOLENT

Serves 8 to 10

3 medium yellow onions, quartered

3 medium carrots, cut into 1-inch
(2.5-centimeter) chunks

8 garlic cloves, coarsely chopped

2 pounds (1 kilogram) chuck roast, stew
meat, or brisket

1½ cups (300 grams) dried beans, such as
kidney, pinto, or cannellini, or a mixture

1 cup (210 grams) pearl barley

1½ pounds (680 grams) Yukon Gold
potatoes, peeled and cut into large
chunks

2 quarts (2 liters) chicken stock or water,
plus more as needed

¼ cup (60 milliliters) pure maple syrup

3 tablespoons (45 milliliters) tomato
paste

2 tablespoons (30 milliliters) soy sauce

2 tablespoons (36 grams) garlic powder

1 tablespoon (15 grams) kosher salt, plus
more to taste

2 teaspoons sweet paprika

1 teaspoon ground cumin

1 teaspoon freshly ground black pepper

Position a rack in the lower third of the oven. Preheat the oven to 200°F (93°C).

Put the onions, carrots, and garlic in a large Dutch oven, followed by the meat. Scatter the beans and barley on top, followed by the potatoes.

Stir together the stock, maple syrup, tomato paste, soy sauce, garlic powder, salt, paprika, cumin, and pepper in a large bowl. Pour the liquid over the contents of the pot and stir once or twice to combine. Place a large piece of parchment paper on top of the pot, cover with a lid, and transfer the pot to the oven.

Cook for about 12 hours, checking now and then to make sure it has enough liquid to just cover. Add small amounts of stock or water as needed. Do not stir the cholent while it cooks; stirring will break up the chunks of potatoes. (If the cholent looks dry after it's finished cooking, add stock or water, 2 cups/480 milliliters at a time, and stir gently to incorporate. Place the pot over low heat on the stovetop and warm until the liquid is gently simmering. You want the stew to be fairly generous in sauce.)

Serve the cholent hot or warm. If not eating right away, let cool, cover, and refrigerate for up to 1 week, or transfer to an airtight container and freeze for up to 3 months.

SLOW COOKER METHOD: To make the cholent in a slow cooker, follow the steps above but place the ingredients in the slow cooker. Cover and cook on Low for 10 to 12 hours.

Chopped Liver?

By Edward Lee

When I was a kid in Canarsie, one of our neighbors—an elderly Jewish woman who lived below us—would watch me when my parents worked late. I can remember with such vividness sitting in her kitchen eating egg noodles, kugels, latkes, and, my personal favorite, chopped-liver sandwiches.

The beauty of a chopped-liver sandwich is that it is the most delicious thing that looks the least appetizing. Its gray-brown color made it seem inedible. My neighbor would spread it thick on rye bread and put a pickle spear on the side. It was textureless and drab. And it would literally melt in my mouth. I loved the rich, buttery flavor with the aftertaste of bitter iron. It was only much later, at a deli, that I realized all those sandwiches I ate as a kid were actually made of chopped liver. What I love about the chopped-liver sandwich is that it is emblematic of all the best Jewish food—frugal, unadorned, nourishing—and it comes with a tinge of guilt if you don't finish every bite on the plate.

As I devoured each bite, I would listen to my neighbor admonish me about my grades and implore me to keep up my piano lessons. Funny thing is, she never told me what I was eating. She would just tell me she was going to make me a sandwich—as if there were no other version of a sandwich that existed on Earth. Maybe there shouldn't be.

$\longrightarrow$

CHOPPED LIVER

Serves 8 as an appetizer

1 pound (455 grams) chicken livers

1 teaspoon kosher salt, plus more to taste

4 tablespoons (60 milliliters) schmaltz (page 238) or olive oil

2 medium onions, halved and thinly sliced (about 1¾ cups/400 grams)

½ teaspoon freshly ground black pepper, plus more to taste

4 large eggs, hard-boiled and cut into ½-inch (1.5-centimeter) chunks

2 tablespoons (6 grams) finely chopped fresh parsley

Lettuce leaves, for serving

Wash the chicken livers in cold water, drain well, and blot dry with paper towels. Season with ½ teaspoon of the salt.

Warm 2 tablespoons (30 milliliters) of the schmaltz in a large skillet over medium heat, until it coats the bottom of the pan when you swirl it, then add the chicken livers. Cook until the livers are cooked on the underside, about 5 minutes. Flip the livers and cook until the other side is cooked, about 5 minutes more. To check for doneness, cut a slit in the middle of a liver with a sharp knife. If the liver is still bloody, cook a bit longer, until it is slightly pink in the middle. Transfer the livers to a bowl and set aside.

In the same skillet, heat the remaining 2 tablespoons (30 milliliters) schmaltz over medium heat. Add the onions, season with the remaining ½ teaspoon salt, and cook until they are soft and caramelized, 30 to 35 minutes.

Place the chicken liver, sautéed onions, and pepper in the bowl of a food processor. Pulse 4 or 5 times to break the liver into smaller pieces. Add the eggs and parsley and pulse a few more times to make a fairly smooth mixture that still has some texture and visible pieces of egg.

Taste and adjust the seasoning, if needed. Serve on a bed of lettuce, if you like, or smeared on bialys (page 36) or sliced challah (page 63) with sour pickle spears (pages 218 and 219).

The chopped liver will keep in an airtight container in the refrigerator for 3 to 4 days or in the freezer for up to 4 months.

Compote

By Shyrla Pakula

As I was making what is probably the five hundredth pot of compote I have cooked since I was a newlywed, it occurred to me that as far as the classic Jewish comfort foods go, compote is pretty much neck and neck with chicken soup (page 74). Sure, it doesn't get the same kudos—it's not a cure-all, it's not "Jewish penicillin"—but it's certainly a lot easier to make, and no animal has to be sacrificed for it.

It's just peeled and cored apples and pears and, if you want to get fancy, maybe strawberries or a cinnamon stick thrown in. No sugar needed. A dash of water, some gentle simmering, and then the

$\longrightarrow$

decision: to blend smooth, or to leave chunky? My mother-in-law favors smooth, especially since she tends to use strawberries, so the result is a pink puree that just slides down. My mother, God rest her soul—who was what we now call a good, plain cook and sure couldn't afford such a luxury as strawberries cooked into compote—left the fruit with a bit of texture. It is this style that I prefer, except when the compote is intended for either the very young or the very old. I've never known a baby to refuse compote, and I know babies. They sit there with their little mouths open, like baby birds, and just scoff it down. Even the most hardened self-feeder relents in the presence of a spoonful of compote—they splash around in it for a bit, perhaps, but eventually, the spoon wins.

Now that I am older and I think of my parents more than ever, I remember my father during his final illness, at home with us for his last weeks, becoming frailer by the day but still clinging to the desire to live. And to eat is to live. But the illness meant he couldn't tolerate lumpy food. Enter my mother-in-law, who has a gift for visiting and nursing the sick, with her smooth, cool compote. Such a simple food, and so delicious. I've got a couple of quarts in my fridge right now—and more in the freezer, for a rainy day.

FRUIT COMPOTE

Serves 4 to 6

2 medium quince

6 cups (1.5 liters) water

¾ cup (150 grams) sugar

¼ cup (60 milliliters) honey

2 strips lemon zest, peeled with a vegetable peeler

Juice of 1 lemon

1 large apple or pear, peeled, quartered, cored, and quarters cut into thirds

1 cinnamon stick (optional)

1 whole clove (optional)

20 dried apricots: 10 left whole, 10 cut in half

Fill a medium bowl with water. Peel the quince, cut them into quarters, remove the hard cores, and cut each quarter into thirds, dropping the prepared pieces into the bowl of water as you work.

Drain the quince and transfer to a medium saucepan. Add the water, ⅓ cup (65 grams) of the sugar, the honey, lemon zest, and lemon juice. Bring to a boil over high heat, then reduce the heat to low, cover, and cook for 1 hour.

Remove the lid and cook until the liquid has reduced by nearly half, about 40 minutes, adding the remaining sugar intermittently, every 10 to 12 minutes (this allows for the slow caramelization of the sugar to transform the quince into a deep, rosy color).

When the quince has noticeably darkened from cooking and caramelization, add the apple, cinnamon stick and clove (if using), and apricots. Add a bit of water if the compote syrup has greatly reduced—it should come about halfway up the fruit in the pot. Cook for about 30 minutes, until the apples have softened and the apricots have plumped but are not falling apart.

Remove the cinnamon stick and clove (if using) and serve warm or at room temperature, with yogurt or spooned over sponge cake, or on its own with a crisp cookie. To store, transfer to a freezer bag or an airtight container and refrigerate for up to 3 weeks, or freeze for up to 3 months.

Concord Grape Juice

| By Rosie Schaap |

For a period that may have lasted just a few weeks, during a summer my family spent on Fire Island in the late 1970s, I'd march off to temple for Shabbat—alone and, in keeping with local custom, barefoot. My mother was suspicious of my sudden, newfound piety but figured it was my way of dealing with my parents' separation. I was no more than eight, and I already understood two things about myself, or at least about my future self: I was a hippie, and I was a Drinker with a capital *D*.

Sure, I liked the whole friendly, beach-casual, liberal-Jew vibe of the place, the guitars and folk songs and earnest long-haired older kids who paid attention to me—all so different from the stuffy Manhattan synagogues I was occasionally dragged to on High Holidays. But the biggest thrill was that I thought I was getting one over: I was sure I was drinking wine (page 278) out of those little Dixie cups. It was, of course, Concord grape juice.

We have the distinctly not-Jewish-sounding Ephraim Wales Bull, who grew the seedling from which the *Vitis labrusca* hybrid was propagated, to thank for the Concord grape. There is, at least, a soupçon of Old Testament pathos in Bull's story. "His discovery enriched others," John Mariani wrote in *The Dictionary of American*

Food and Drink, "but not himself: his gravestone reads, 'He sowed, but others reaped.'"

Many of the kosher wines served at the Seders of my youth were made from Concord grapes and were unpleasantly sweet. I say this even as an unrepentant wino: Where the juice of the Concord grape is concerned, I still prefer it unfermented. Such is the power of faith—or at least of a child's capacity for magical thinking—that I got pretty drunk off the stuff anyway, and still do.

Cottage Cheese

By Gabriella Gershenson

The iconic version, served in a hollowed-out cantaloupe at your local diner, is supposedly the option for people who make sacrifices for their waistlines. But whoever designated cottage cheese as such is clearly not Jewish, because we choose our appetites over our waistlines every time. To us, cottage cheese isn't diet food. It's the New World version of pot cheese, curd cheese, or *tvorog*, as my Soviet Jewish immigrant family calls it. It's richer, tangier, more arid, and denser than the drippy, lumpy American stuff. After emigrating from Russia to Massachusetts, my paternal grandfather still made his fresh, the whey in his fridge proof that the curds were his own. My mother's mother, from Riga, Latvia, would often eat store-bought cottage cheese on bread for lunch (the original ricotta toast?), a version of a meal that has sustained Latvians, both Jewish and non-Jewish, for generations. If you think cottage cheese is starting to sound more Eastern European than Jewish, try making kugel (page 171) without it.

Cream Cheese

By Gabriella Gershenson

You can't stuff a cheese blintz without it. It's the vital ingredient in rugelach dough. It inspires allegiances (see the cult classic Temp Tee) as well as mutiny (ugh, tofu cream cheese). It's a natural mate for lox, the ultimate Ashkenazi delicacy. When slathered on a bagel, it's what much of the world, for better or worse, thinks of as Jewish food. Though cream cheese is an American invention, it was put to best culinary use by Jewish immigrants, who, according to food historian Gil Marks, swapped in the thick, tangy dairy product for pot cheese in traditional Eastern European recipes. But since Breakstone's and Philadelphia were *not* the curd cheese of the old country, cream cheese was also the catalyst for some key Jewish American innovations, most notably the New York–style cheesecake (page 68). Like the enterprising Jews who raised the ingredient to lofty heights, it's eminently adaptable—maybe even *too* adaptable, as anyone who's ever grimaced at Oreo or jalapeño cream cheese knows.

$\longrightarrow$

CREAM CHEESE

Makes 4 to 4½ cups (600 to 675 grams)

4 cups (1 liter) heavy cream

4 cups (1 liter) whole milk, ideally raw

¼ teaspoon mesophilic cheese culture (can be purchased online)

4 drops liquid vegetable rennet (can be purchased at specialty grocers or online), diluted in 2 tablespoons water

½ teaspoon sea salt, plus more to taste

Pour the heavy cream and milk into a large pot and heat over medium-high heat to 75°F (24°C).

Turn off the heat and sprinkle the cheese culture on top. Allow it to sit, undisturbed, for 5 minutes; the culture is activated by the heat. Add the rennet-water solution and stir gently up and down and side to side—no more than four to six gentle stirs—to disperse the culture and the rennet.

Loosely cover the pot with a clean kitchen towel or a couple layers of cheesecloth and let sit for 12 to 14 hours, until it has thickened; when you gently shift the pot back and forth, the mixture should look like very loose panna cotta. How long this takes will depend on the temperature of your kitchen—the cooler the kitchen, the longer it will take. Conversely, the warmer the kitchen, the faster it will occur. Gently stir in the salt.

Line a strainer with a couple layers of fine cheesecloth and set it over a bowl to catch the whey. Carefully pour the cream mixture into the strainer. It may look more watery than you expect it to, but that is OK. Strain the cheese, without pressing it through the strainer, for about 5 hours, until the paste looks drier and much more like cream cheese—the portion of cheese on the periphery, closer to the cloth and strainer, should be drier, and the center, wetter. If it is particularly warm in your kitchen and the cheese seems too liquid, refrigerate the cheese for several hours or up to overnight to help it set before continuing.

To further strain the cheese, gather the ends of the cheesecloth, tie them to make a bundle, and hang the bundle—either from an upper cabinet with a bowl below to catch the excess whey or by placing a wooden spoon across the opening of a carafe and hanging the sack of cream cheese from the spoon so it drains into the carafe. Either way, you want to utilize gravity to help extract the remaining fluid from the cheese. Strain for 5 to 6 hours more, until the cream is stiffer and no longer loose and runny.

You'll find that the layer of cheese closest to the fabric will strain before the more interior parts. Aid the straining of whey by gently turning and stirring the cheese within the cloth so that wetter parts of the cheese can also strain.

When your cream cheese is at the right consistency for your schmearing preferences, taste it and season with additional salt, if needed.

The cream cheese will keep in an airtight container in the refrigerator for up to 1 week. Spread it on bialys (page 36) or bagels, and serve alongside home-cured gravlax (page 184).

Dates

By Adeena Sussman

Ever since biblical times, when the image of a date palm was etched on Israelite currency, the fruit borne by those majestic, flowering trees has been in high demand. According to tradition, the nectar promised to Moses in a "land flowing with milk and honey" was in fact date syrup, establishing the fruit it was made from as a delicacy with no equal. That's certainly the case in modern-day Israel, where dates—many cultivated locally—are prized stock. In the Carmel Market in Tel Aviv, they're priced according to their size, with the largest and most expensive clocking in at about 80 shekels per kilo (about 11 dollars per pound). Tourists buy boxes of luxurious Medjools for gifts, and Israelis seek them out for special occasions, but locals often turn to a paler, smaller offering, the Deglet Noor. If the Medjool, with its meltingly thin skin and dense, fudgy interior, is the couture gown of the category, then the Deglet Noor, which is smaller and cheaper, is a more modest, ready-to-wear frock. I love nothing better than ending a Shabbat meal with glasses of steaming-hot mint tea and *ja'aleh*, a platter of nuts and dried fruits served by Arabs and North African Jews alike.

A MEMORABLE END TO A MEAL

The word *ja'aleh* is Arabic for "gratification," and the lavish array of nuts, fruits, and roasted beans that goes by this name delivers on its promise. The custom of *ja'aleh* is derived from the ancient Greek practice of eating fruit before a meal, which has been sustained to this day by Yemenite Jews. An assortment of dried fruit, nuts, and roasted beans is enjoyed before Shabbat dinner, at the end, or both. In Israel, where there is a significant Yemenite Jewish population, the tradition has also been adopted by non-Yemenites, with trays of nuts, fruit, and other sweets capping a meal—and not only on Shabbat. *Ja'aleh* can look like a trail mix, with ingredients all jumbled together, or take the form of an extravagant platter bearing a cornucopia of goodies. You can have an all-nut *ja'aleh* with savory spices, or one that includes confections like halvah (page 124), *mamoul* (date cookies), and Turkish delight (admittedly an unorthodox interpretation). Some hosts roast and season their own nuts, while most take the opportunity to present what is essentially a store-bought dessert that is easy and impressive. To create a stunning effect, cluster fruit and nuts separately on your favorite tray to create a look of abundance. Think nuts in their shells, dates and raisins on the stem, plump dried figs, dried red plums, a tangerine with the leaf attached, and crystallized ginger, to name a few possibilities. A cup of fresh mint tea or Yemenite white coffee (a brew with aromatic spices, such as hawaij, cardamom, cinnamon, and ginger) is a perfect accompaniment.

Deli

By David Sax

In the years since I wrote a book on Jewish delicatessens, I have constantly been asked, "What's the best _____?" by deli lovers. What's the best deli worldwide, in New York, in America? What's the best sandwich? Who has the best pastrami? And on and on. No matter how often I try to deflect that tired, thoughtless question ("There is no objective best," "Each deli specializes in something unique that can't be compared," "I don't have a favorite child, and I don't have a favorite deli"), people just nod their heads, ignore every word, and then say, "Yes, but which is the *best*?" They will not accept subtlety. They demand certainty. Context is nice. Storytelling is great. But let's skip the history lesson, you say, and get to what is the tastiest, most *geshmack* thing I can put in my mouth.

I will answer your question, but I will not be happy doing it.

A delicatessen menu is like the "greatest hits" album of centuries of Yiddish cuisine. It's the assimilated, economically viable foods that have been shaped to Diaspora tastes (sandwiches, big portions, lots of fries), and not the stuffed goose necks or lung-and-liver scrambles your greenhorn grandparents ate a century ago. What is deli food fundamentally? It's what you go to a deli for. You don't go to a deli for the sides (sorry, kasha, kishke, knishes, kreplach, and other beige foods that start with *k*). Same with coleslaw and pickles. "A deli should serve matzo ball soup!" That's the taste of Friday nights at Mom's table, not a restaurant.

$\longrightarrow$

No, a deli exists to serve delicatessen, the cured meats of the American Ashkenazi immigrant experience. Forget turkey (a dry leftover of 1980s fat scares) and roast beef (the most goyish cold cut). No dice, either, for hard-to-find regional meats, including rolled beef, salt beef, karnatzel, and baby beef. Forget the ubiquitous garlic salami and its variants.

So what we are really talking about here is a battle between corned beef and pastrami, the competing poles of deli's fleishig soul. Between the pickled brisket and the peppery, smoky navel. Both are the core of any deli. Both have regional allegiances (pastrami is more coastal, corned beef more Midwestern). Either goes perfectly with rye and mustard.

But if, like poor Sophie, I could choose only one, then I would begrudgingly take pastrami. Why? Because pastrami captures the imagination and fires up a passion in a way that even the best corned beef doesn't. Pastrami is a challenge to make, and is not known for its subtlety. Pastrami is the fire and brimstone of the Torah. Corned beef is the wisdom of the Talmud. Pastrami is more pan-Judaic than corned beef. It came to Romania by way of Turkey and possibly even Mongolian horsemen. Pastrami has consequences. It can leave you feeling ecstatic or like garbage, or a guilt- and pleasure-inducing combination of both, which is a fitting metaphor for the Jewish experience, isn't it?

Dill

By Eve Jochnowitz

Dill (*Anethum graveolens*) might be the seasoning that most characteristically delivers a *Yidishn tam*, that ineffable flavor of Jewishness, to a dish. Boiled potatoes without dill are so forlorn as to be unimaginable, and fresh and pickled cucumbers rely so heavily on this herb that the Yiddish names for dill (according to Nahum Stutchkoff's thesaurus, *Der Oytser fun der Yidisher Shprakh*) include *ugerke groz* (cucumber grass) and *ugerke grins* (cucumber greens), along with *krop*, *krip*, *ukrop*, *ukrip*, and *koper*. Mushrooms, fish, buttermilk soup, and, of course, chicken soup and vegetarian approximations of chicken soup all require dill to lighten, sharpen, and enliven their flavors and aromas.

The Jews of Eastern and Central Europe may have learned their enthusiasm for dill from their neighbors (the peregrinating epicure Joseph Wechsberg wrote that it is possible the Poles "overdo the dill business"), but they made the herb their own by incorporating it into uniquely Jewish ceremonial dishes like *di goldene yoykh*, the rich chicken soup served at weddings and Sabbath feasts.

Plus, Marlene Dietrich said, "Dill is the most important of all herbs."

Eggplant

By Gabriela Geselowitz

As the potato (page 226) is to Ashkenazim, the eggplant is to Sephardim.

The eggplant is hearty and easily prepared in many ways: stewed, stuffed, pickled, roasted, pureed, you name it. The berry (yes, technically, that's what it is) is so ubiquitous in Jewish cuisine that there's a classic Ladino song in which the tomato and eggplant verbally battle for vegetable supremacy. According to the late Jewish food expert Gil Marks, the tribe is somewhat responsible for eggplant's popularity. Though the eggplant originated in India, Arabs brought it to Spain, where it became a dietary staple. And so when Jews were eventually expelled, they took their eggplant recipes with them, and the rest, as they say, is history.

AZERBAIJANI EGGPLANT SALAD
by Joan Nathan

Serves 6 to 8

2 medium eggplant, halved lengthwise

4 or 5 small tomatoes

2 red bell peppers

2 garlic cloves, coarsely chopped

½ bunch fresh cilantro or parsley, chopped

2 tablespoons (30 milliliters) extra-virgin olive oil

Juice of ½ lemon, plus more as needed

Kosher salt and freshly ground black pepper

½ teaspoon harissa, homemade (page 291) or store-bought

Warm pita or other bread, for serving

Position the top oven rack 8 inches (20 centimeters) away from the broiler. Preheat the broiler. Line a baking sheet with aluminum foil.

Place the eggplant on the baking sheet, cut-side down, followed by the tomatoes and bell peppers. Broil, checking every few minutes, until the eggplant and peppers are charred and softened; it should take about 15 minutes for the tomatoes to start to char and their skins to crack, 15 minutes for the peppers, and 25 to 30 minutes for the eggplant. You may need to turn the peppers over once to make sure they are evenly charred.

Put the eggplant in a colander in the sink to drain; set the tomatoes aside to cool. Put the peppers in a large bowl and cover the top of the bowl with plastic wrap or a wide plate to steam (this will allow you to easily remove the skins). This should all take about 30 minutes. Drain the excess juice off the vegetables and peel them. Seed the tomatoes and peppers and cut one of the peppers into strips.

Place the eggplant, tomatoes, peppers (except the pepper strips), and garlic in the bowl of a food processor. Pulse briefly, just until the mixture is chunky—texture is key. Stir in all but a few tablespoons of the cilantro, the olive oil, and the lemon juice. Taste and season with salt and black pepper, then taste again and adjust the seasonings if needed, adding more lemon juice if the flavors need to be brighter. Stir in the harissa.

Spoon the salad into a bowl, top with the pepper strips, and sprinkle with the remaining cilantro. Serve with warm pita or other bread on the side.

Entenmann's

By Phil Rosenthal

I grew up in New York, and both of my parents worked, so I would be alone from about 3:00 to 5:30 every day after school. There was always a box of those chocolate-covered Entenmann's doughnuts in the house, and the first thing I did when I got home was have a doughnut with a glass of milk. I would break the doughnut in half so I could dunk it in the milk. Then I would watch TV: the '70s game shows—*Match Game*, *Hollywood Squares*, *The Joker's Wild*—and then the TV movie.

It's such a happy memory. I didn't care that I was alone since I had those doughnuts.

Every region has its own thing, a shared food history. My wife grew up in Philadelphia, and for her it was Tastykakes. In the New York area, especially if you were Jewish, you had Entenmann's dough-nuts. That was before Entenmann's got kosher certification, which happened in the '80s. After that, the connection was complete.

I don't know the last time I had an Entenmann's doughnut. These days, if I have a doughnut, it's not going to be from a box.

One time, my daughter visited my parents, and her grandpa offered her an Entenmann's chocolate doughnut. She said she had never seen one before, and I was shocked. She tried it, and I was so touched by how much she liked it.

Certain things are eternal that way—they bring you right back to childhood.

Eyerlekh

By Barbara Kirshenblatt-Gimblett

In the days when my mother and paternal grandmother would buy the whole chicken from the kosher butcher—my mother was from Brisk (Brześć nad Bugiem), in what is now Belarus, and my grandmother was from Apt (Opatów), Poland—they would get *everything*: The feet were essential for the chicken soup (you had to clip the claws and scrape off the outer yellow skin with boiling water) and beloved for their rubbery texture, the best part being the "palm" of the foot. The *helzl* (neck) was its own delicacy, both the *gorgl* (neck bones), which went into the soup, and the skin, which was stuffed with flour and chopped chicken fat, the ends stitched closed with white cotton thread, and roasted with the chicken to golden-crisp perfection. In the old country, once you sucked all the goodness from the neck bones, you could take them apart and use them to play jacks.

Then there were the treasures inside the chicken: the *pipek* (gizzard), chicken liver, heart, and—treasure of treasures—the *eyerlekh*, or what we called eggies. To be technical, they are oocytes, on their way to becoming the eggs with whites and shells that hens will lay. Drop them into *di goldene yoykh*, the golden broth otherwise known as chicken soup, and they solidify into the most delicate and delectable pale yellow yolks. As children growing up in downtown Toronto's immigrant neighborhood, my siblings and I fought over them. The chicken might have two feet, but it never had enough eyerlekh, and my mother would parcel them out carefully as we kids made our own calculations. Eventually, she gave in to our pleas and asked the butcher for several necks and extra eyerlekh, although this always seemed to me like cheating.

Today eyerlekh are nowhere to be found—almost. Not in the supermarket nor at the butchers, and not even in Poland, where it is illegal to sell them today because, I was told, they cannot be tested for salmonella. But they can still be bought in New York's Chinatown, where nothing inside the chicken goes to waste. And they have been rediscovered by experimental chefs, notably Dan Barber of Blue Hill in New York. Nothing, however, will ever compare with the delicate flavor and texture of eyerlekh gently poached in di goldene yoykh.

Flanken

By Michael Wex

Known as "short ribs" in standard English, flanken are a tough cut of meat, heavy on tendon and fat. Given the frequency with which signs posting this week's price used to appear in the windows of kosher butcher shops, flanken occupy surprisingly little space in older Jewish cookbooks, many of which don't even accord them the dignity of a freestanding dish but simply list them, often as no more than a possible ingredient, in recipes for mushroom-barley soup, borscht, the weekly cholent, or anywhere else where they could stew long enough to be chewable. Just as the Yiddish from which they get their name was said to be *red zikh aleyn*—to issue naturally from a Jewish mouth without any of the study or instruction needed for Hebrew—so flanken, *heymish* and hearty as they are, were thought to leap into that mouth with nothing but common sense as a guide. The name itself has the kind of clunky, endearingly awkward charm more redolent of home ec than of haute cuisine, and cookbooks with detailed instructions for preparing brain fritters or lung and liver seem to have assumed that anyone who could boil water didn't need any help with flanken.

But sooner or later, America works its magic, the culinary orientalism endemic to American Jewry kicks in, and flanken forsake the workaday pots we thought they loved for the more upscale ambience of the kosher or kosher-style buffet. Rebranded as the less overtly Jewish Miami ribs, these faux–Far Eastern flanken are marinated in some combination of sesame oil, Worcestershire sauce, plum sauce, soy sauce, hoisin, and oyster sauce, then quickly grilled. Kashrut embraces Korean kalbi—as long as the oyster sauce is fake—at weddings, bar mitzvahs, and fund-raising dinners, while a still, small voice whispers, "Flanken, flanken," to those in the know.

→

BUT DON'T EAT TOO MUCH!

Every Fourth of July, competitive eaters head to Coney Island in Brooklyn to see who can consume the most hot dogs and buns in one sitting. But did you know that the world of competitive eating has lesser-known contests, including some with kosher food? We're talking matzo balls and hamantaschen. Which begs the gluttonous question: What would be the toughest kosher or culturally Jewish food to eat in mass quantities? Kosher culinary experts—and some comedians—weigh in.

"What comes to my mind right away is flanken, which, by the way, is flanken delicious," comedian Elon Gold said. "But just the bones would be a problem." He considered the question again. "*Maror.* Where's the *maror*-eating contest where everybody's eyes start tearing up?"

Elan Kornblum, president and publisher of *Great Kosher Restaurants* magazine, opted for a different Passover food: *shmurah matzo.* "After a while, it would be very dry," he said. "I think I could eat maybe three or four."

Michael Gershkovich, owner and executive chef of Mike's Bistro in New York City, said shmurah matzo is too dangerous and shouldn't be allowed in an eating contest. Instead he went with *yapchik,* a hearty dish with potato kugel and flanken or other meat. Talk about heavy lifting.

Wandering Que owner and pitmaster Ari White said he'd go with *ptcha* (page 228), a dish made from jellied calves' feet, or possibly chopped liver (page 85): "I wouldn't want to be the guy that put seven years of cholesterol in my body in one sitting."

Mendy Merel, owner of Mendy's (of *Seinfeld* fame), has some experience in this field. "We did have a matzo ball–eating contest once," he said. "One guy ate twenty, and I think he didn't go to the bathroom for two weeks."

Chef and *Joy of Kosher* author Jamie Geller said it is a joy to eat cholent, but not too much of it. "One time I was judging a contest and after having a spoon or two of twelve different cholents, I was already dying," she said. "I think a normal person could eat three bowls at most. I don't know how many a competitive eater could eat."

Isaac Bernstein, culinary director of Pomegranate Supermarket in Brooklyn, said *gribenes* (page 120) would be tough to eat in a large quantity. "A pound of it would kill you."

Alan Zeitlin

FLANKEN

4 pounds (1.8 kg) bone-in beef short ribs, cut flanken-style (see Note)

¾ cup (180 milliliters) brewed espresso or very strong coffee

¾ cup (180 milliliters) blackstrap molasses

½ cup (120 milliliters) apple cider vinegar

⅓ cup (80 milliliters) tomato paste

⅓ cup (80 milliliters) pomegranate molasses

1 teaspoon kosher salt

1 teaspoon ground ginger

½ teaspoon freshly ground black pepper

1 cinnamon stick

3 whole cloves

Zest and juice of 1 large orange

Put the ribs in a large pot, cover with cold water, and bring to a boil over high heat. Reduce the heat to low, cover, and simmer for about 30 minutes, or until the meat is just starting to become fork-tender. Drain the ribs (discard the cooking liquid) and transfer to a 9 by 13-inch (23 by 33-centimeter) baking dish. Set aside.

Combine the espresso, blackstrap molasses, vinegar, tomato paste, pomegranate molasses, salt, ginger, pepper, cinnamon stick, and cloves in a medium saucepan. Add the orange juice to the mixture (reserve the zest); stir to combine. Bring the mixture to a boil over medium-high heat.

Reduce the heat to medium-low and simmer gently until the sauce has thickened considerably and coats the back of the spoon, 15 to 20 minutes. Remove from the heat, discard the cinnamon stick and cloves, and stir in the orange zest. Pour the sauce over the ribs, turning to coat. Let cool to room temperature, then cover with plastic wrap and refrigerate for at least 4 hours and up to overnight.

Preheat the oven to 325°F (163°C).

Discard the plastic wrap and cover the dish tightly with aluminum foil. Bake for about 30 minutes, then turn the ribs over and bake, uncovered, basting now and again, for about 45 minutes, or until the meat is nearly falling off the bone and the sauce has thickened.

Serve the ribs immediately, family-style, drizzled with the sauce.

NOTE: Flanken-style ribs are cut across the bone (not between the bones), resulting in longer, narrower strips of meat with several pieces of bone across them.

Flódni

By Ráchel Raj

The essence of *flódni* is that it's a kind of comfort food—a vehicle through which the Jewish mother can extend the fullness of her love. It's not a smothering love, but a generous love. There are those who'll assign symbolic significance to the cake's various layers—the apple, the walnut, the poppy seed, and the plum jam—but I'm not of that school. I hold that the key to flódni is that it is filled with the richest, most delicious things a Jewish mother can offer.

Though not originally Hungarian—the cake's roots trace back to the heart of Ashkenaz around the year 1000 (from the Yiddish *fluden*, from the German *fladen*, for "flat")—the cake took up residence in the Hungarian-speaking world in the nineteenth century and has flourished there ever since.

The time and effort involved in making flódni is immense. Each of the fillings has to be prepared separately; the dough has to be rolled out. The assembly is labor-intensive. Just peeling the apples can be a multi-hour process. There are those who might say that it's too much or too rich, but it's not true. The key to the cake is its harmony. The fillings don't overwhelm one another. Everything serves a purpose: The poppy seed offers an earthiness; the walnuts, a sweetness; the apples, a tartness. And the plum adds flavor. Together, they form a unified whole.

Gefilte Fish

By Éric Ripert

It's not as bad as it's made out to be!

I've been invited by friends many times over the years to celebrate Shabbat and Passover, and gefilte fish is always served. When I first tried it, friends warned me that it tasted like a bad pike quenelle—so naturally, I had pretty low expectations. But I've been pleasantly surprised on many occasions. When prepared properly, gefilte fish is moist, light, and full of flavor.

CARPS FOR KIDS

The Carp in the Bathtub is, of course, the greatest work of children's literature ever written about gefilte fish. Originally published in 1972, it tells the tale of a daring quest to rescue a fish before it is gefilted. Barbara Cohen's story, set in 1930s Brooklyn, is atmospheric and funny and deliciously illustrated by Joan Halpern in wavy-lined, stripey, pointillist, slightly psychedelic black-and-white style.

The story: Every year before Passover, Mama brings home a live carp and keeps it in the tub for a week, so it will be extra fresh and tasty when served at the Seder. One year, nine-year-old Leah and her brother, Harry, feel that this season's carp is special: friendlier and shinier and more bright-eyed than past carps. He even swims to the edge of the tub to visit the children whenever they enter the bathroom. Cohen writes: "Every time Harry or I had to go to the toilet, we would grab a crust of bread or a rusty lettuce leaf from the kitchen. While we sat on the toilet, we fed the bread or the lettuce leaf to the carp. This made going to the bathroom really fun, instead of just a waste of time."

The kids name the carp Joe and resolve to save him, hiding him temporarily in their recently widowed neighbor Mrs. Ginzburg's tub. Alas, their father orders them to bring Joe back, despite their big "fish are friends, not food" pitch. "It's your mother's fish and it cost her a lot of money," he tells them. They return the fish. Their mother kills it. This is a metaphor for the powerlessness of childhood. "We cried ourselves to sleep that night, and the next night, too. Then we made ourselves stop crying. After that, we felt as if we were years older than Mama and Papa." This is a good lesson! Sometimes life is unfair, and we have to suck it up, like a filter feeder.

Thankfully, Papa understands the kids' grief, and he gets them a cat.

Out of print for years (I blame the vegetarians and helicopter parents), *The Carp in the Bathtub* was republished by Kar-Ben in 2016; you should absolutely possess it, whether you have children or not. It is notable, however, that the greatest work of children's literature ever written about gefilte fish does not actually involve eating gefilte fish.

Marjorie Ingall

⟶

GEFILTE FISH

Makes 14 patties; serves 6 to 8

FOR THE POACHING BROTH

12 cups (3 liters) water

¾ cup (180 milliliters) dry white wine

1 medium carrot, coarsely chopped

1 celery stalk, coarsely chopped

1 medium yellow onion, coarsely chopped

1 leek, white and light green parts only, coarsely chopped

1 teaspoon whole black peppercorns

5 sprigs thyme

2 teaspoons kosher salt

1 garlic clove, smashed

2 bay leaves

1 tablespoon (15 milliliters) fresh lemon juice

½ cup (28 grams) packed fresh flat-leaf parsley leaves and stems

FOR THE GEFILTE FISH

1½ medium carrots

1 medium yellow onion, cut into chunks

1 pound (455 grams) skinless white-fleshed fish fillets, such as cod, striped bass, carp, pike, or halibut

½ pound (227 grams) skinless salmon fillets

2 large eggs, beaten

5 tablespoons (40 grams) matzo meal

2 teaspoons vegetable oil

2 teaspoons kosher salt

¼ teaspoon freshly ground black pepper

1 teaspoon lemon zest

Make the poaching broth: Combine all the broth ingredients in a Dutch oven or other large, deep pot. Bring to a boil over high heat, then reduce the heat to medium-low, cover with the lid ajar, and simmer for 30 minutes, skimming the surface occasionally to remove any impurities. Strain the broth through a fine-mesh sieve set over a large bowl. Discard the solids and return the broth to the pot. Cover and set aside.

Make the gefilte fish: Cut the half carrot into chunks. Place the carrot chunks and onion in the bowl of a food processor and pulse until the vegetables are finely chopped, being careful not to liquefy them. Transfer the vegetables to a large bowl. Working in two batches, place the fish in the food processor and process until it is finely chopped but not mushy, then transfer it to the bowl with the carrot and onion.

Add the eggs, matzo meal, vegetable oil, salt, pepper, and lemon zest and stir well to combine.

Return the poaching broth to a simmer over medium-low heat. Rinse your hands in a bowl of cold water and shape a heaping ¼ cup (about 72 grams) of the fish mixture into an oval-shaped patty. Set the patty aside on a plate and repeat with the remaining fish mixture.

Lower the remaining whole carrot and the fish patties into the broth using a slotted spoon (depending on the size of your pot, you may have to do this in two or three batches; you don't want the patties to crowd one another). Cover and simmer for 20 minutes, until the patties are firm and cooked through (when you cut one in half, the center should be opaque). Remove the carrot and the patties from the pot and transfer to a plate to cool. If cooking in batches, repeat with the remaining patties. Once the carrot is cool enough to handle, slice it into thin rounds.

Serve the gefilte fish warm or at room temperature, topped with the sliced carrot rounds and with horseradish (page 141) on the side. If you're making the gefilte fish ahead of time, allow the patties to cool in a large container, then submerge them in the cooled poaching broth and refrigerate for up to 2 days until ready to serve.

Goose

By Jeffrey Yoskowitz

If you asked Yidn from the Old Country about their most delectable, ultimately special meal, the answer would most certainly have included goose. Goose was the aspirational Eastern and Central European Jewish protein. Not chicken. Not beef. In Romania, Jews made that now famous pastrami we associate with Jewish deli by curing goose meat, then rubbing it with spices, then smoking it. Roasted goose was the coveted main during German and Eastern European Hanukkah feasts, with potato latkes fried in the goose's fat served alongside it. The liver from the Hanukkah goose (aka foie gras) was usually stored for Passover.

Goose was a central feature of Yiddish culture and its food traditions. In a classic Sholem Aleichem story from 1902 fittingly titled

"Geese," the female Jewish protagonist takes the reader through the process of purchasing young geese in October and fattening them up for winter for their meat, fat, and down feathers.

The realities of twentieth-century America, however, forever altered Jewish eating. Beef was cheap. Chicken was even cheaper. In 1948, A&P supermarkets hosted the "Chicken of Tomorrow" contest to develop a new breed of chicken—pretty close to what we're eating today. Unlike geese, the chicken of tomorrow could be held in captivity and fed nothing but corn and grain. Stalwart Jewish goose lovers attempted illegally raising geese in their tenement backyards in the Lower East Side, but eventually the forceful powers of Americanization (and sanitation) won out.

As industrial farming took root, goose went from being the choice meat of the Jewish community to a relic of the Old World, something referenced by cranky old Jewish men lamenting the state of the world, an erstwhile Dickens novel or Sholem Aleichem story. But that shouldn't negate the importance of geese to Jewish gastronomic history.

Gribenes

By Joshua Malina

Mine eyes smell onions: I shall weep anon.
—*William Shakespeare*

But these are the onions of gribenes; and my tears signal joy!
—*Joshua Malina*

For me, the sine qua non of Jewish food would have to be *gribenes*. They are deceptively simple fare—chicken (or goose) skin and onions fried in chicken fat (see page 238). You can't go wrong with these ingredients. The snack's origin is shrouded in mystery, but apparently it all began somewhere in medieval Germany. I picture the shtetl version of the invention of Reese's peanut butter cups. A Teutonic balaboosta was rendering goose fat, when—oy!—some onions fell into the pan, and the kosher version of pork rinds was born.

My own connection to the food goes back to my childhood. My paternal grandma, Jean Malina—*aleha ha-shalom*—used to make gribenes as a treat every Pesach. My family would arrive for Seder, and she would take me aside and hand me a plastic container filled to the brim with crispy goodness. I was then left to dispense the tasty morsels to the rest of the *mishpacha*. That I was given container privileges is my strongest argument that I was her favorite.

I didn't start cooking myself until my wife, Melissa, got pregnant, so—to my great regret—I didn't learn to prepare gribenes at Grandma Jean's side. But I do consider it a tribute to her memory when I make them every Pesach. I like to think that the fumes reach up to Gan Eden, and she knows she's remembered with love.

Want to make them yourself? You'll need a pound of chicken skin with a little fat on it (two pounds is twice as good). This you should accumulate during the year, when you make soup. Cut the skin into small pieces and place it in a pan over low heat. Salt it, add a tablespoon of water, and cook for about 20 minutes. When the fat starts to render, toss in a couple of chopped-up onions and cook until crispy. It takes a long time! Read a good book.

For an elegant vegetarian version, simply don't eat anything at all.

If gribenes be the food of love, fry on!

Halvah

By Molly Yeh

There's simply no such thing as too much halvah. It keeps forever in the freezer; is typically made from tahini, sugar, and little else; complies with basically every dietary need or law; and is delicious. The name is derived from the Arabic word *halwa*, meaning "sweetmeat," and it is believed to have originated in Turkey as a flour-and-sugar-based candy. As it spread throughout the Middle East and Asia, variations made with other ingredients like ground nuts, seeds, carrots, and semolina were popularized.

In the early twentieth century, a sesame-based version enjoyed by Ashkenazi Jews in Eastern Europe made its way to Brooklyn when the entrepreneur Nathan Radutzky founded Joyva, the largest and oldest halvah producer in the States. His products grace the shelves of practically every deli and kosher grocery section in the country.

Halvah may look like a bar of soap, but it is, in fact, a heavenly confection that crumbles like the innards of a Butterfinger and shaves like Parmesan. You either love it or you're completely indifferent to it: It's either a hard yes any time the word *halvah* is in front of the words *sundae*, *sufganiyot*, or *French toast* on a menu, or it's just a brown brick of unglamorous candy that's a Purim basket space-filler getting between you and the chocolate.

If you identify with the latter, it's OK. Really. It's probably just a matter of time until you cross paths with life-changing halvah. Either that or you're a monster with immature taste buds who wouldn't know a culinary masterpiece if it hit you in the face. That's all.

HALVAH GOES ARTISANAL

Joyva has been producing halvah in their Brooklyn warehouse since 1907 and today ships more than 35,000 pounds of the nutty confection each week to supermarkets, Middle Eastern and health food shops, and stores that cater to kosher customers. Overseeing production is Richard Radutzky, the grandson of Joyva's founder, Nathan Radutzky.

In the past few years, however, the sesame world has welcomed new, promising companies like Soom Foods, founded by sisters Shelby and Amy Zitelman and Jackie Horvitz, which produces tahini made from an Ethiopian variety of sesame seeds called white humera, and Seed + Mill, which sells tahini, halvah, and sesame spices at Chelsea Market in New York City.

If Joyva is the Heinz ketchup of sesame, the Soom Sisters, as they call themselves, want to be POM Wonderful, the company that helped vault the exotic Mediterranean pomegranate (page 223) into the health-conscious mainstream. "Sesame seeds have long been a part of American cuisine because they top hamburger buns and bagels, but they are just emerging as a super seed, filled with protein, calcium, omega-3 fatty acids, and important minerals," said Amy.

Leah Koenig

⟶

MARBLE HALVAH

Makes one 3½ by 7-inch (9 by 18-centimeter) loaf; serves 10 to 12

2 cups (400 grams) sugar

½ cup (120 milliliters) water

1 teaspoon pure vanilla extract

1½ cups (360 milliliters) tahini, at room temperature

¼ teaspoon kosher salt

¼ cup (74 grams) Nutella

Line a 3½ by 7-inch (9 by 18-centimeter) loaf pan (or a pan of a similar size) with parchment paper, leaving 1 inch (2.5 centimeters) of parchment overhanging on two sides.

Combine the sugar, water, and vanilla in a medium saucepan fitted with a candy thermometer. Heat over medium-high heat, stirring, until the sugar has dissolved, then cook, without stirring, until the mixture reaches 245°F (118°C), 15 to 20 minutes.

Meanwhile, in the bowl of a stand mixer fitted with the paddle attachment, combine the tahini and salt. If there are any lumps in the tahini or if it has separated, stir by hand until it's smooth. Have the Nutella standing by near the mixer, ideally in an ice cream scoop with a trigger release so that it can be added as quickly as possible.

When the sugar mixture reaches 245°F (118°C), turn the mixer on low speed and carefully pour the sugar syrup into the bowl and mix for no more than 15 to 20 seconds, until just combined. Immediately add the Nutella and mix for just two or three revolutions of the paddle, so the Nutella creates a marbled effect, then turn off the mixer and quickly use a rubber spatula to scrape the mixture into the prepared loaf pan. Smooth out the top with the spatula as best as you can. Allow the halvah to harden at room temperature for at least 30 minutes.

Use the overhanging parchment to remove the halvah from the pan and serve.

The halvah will keep wrapped in plastic wrap at room temperature for several weeks.

Hamantaschen

By Marjorie Ingall

Yay, the heritage cookie of the "they tried to kill us, we won, let's eat" narrative! The name literally means "Haman's pockets" (not "Haman's hat," as it is usually translated), after the villain of the Purim story, and probably comes from an eighteenth-century German snack cake called *Mohntaschen—Mohn* means "poppy seed," and *Taschen* means "pockets." Hamantaschen, therefore, is a play on words (and you know how we Jews love those). In Israel, they're known as *oznei Haman*, "Haman's ears," perhaps derived from the medieval Italian custom of cutting off a criminal's ears before hanging him. (You know how we Jews love dark humor.)

Whatever the origin, they're delicious. That is, when made correctly. Friends—perhaps under the influence of a great deal of alcohol, another delightful Purim custom—can come to blows about whether the poppy seed (page 224) ur-filling is delicious or disgusting, and whether the dough should be made with cream cheese (page 93), oil, or butter. Traditionalists think prune and apricot are already a pox on Jewish history; modernists embrace fillings ranging from salted caramel to s'mores to cardamom pear and goat cheese to Funfetti cheesecake to gummy worms. Hamantaschen, like everything else, are crafted in our own self-image.

→

HAMANTASCHEN

Makes about 32 cookies

FOR THE FILLING

2 cups (340 grams) pitted prunes

Finely grated zest of 1 lemon

2 tablespoons (30 milliliters) fresh lemon juice

¼ teaspoon kosher salt

1 cup (240 milliliters) water

½ cup (50 grams) sugar

FOR THE DOUGH

2½ cups (315 grams) unbleached all-purpose flour

¼ cup (50 grams) sugar

⅛ teaspoon kosher salt

8 tablespoons (1 stick/115 grams) cold unsalted butter, cut into bits

½ (4-ounce/115-gram) package cream cheese, cut into bits

1 large egg

1 teaspoon pure vanilla extract

Make the filling: Combine the prunes, lemon zest, lemon juice, salt, and water in a medium saucepan. Bring to a boil over medium heat and cook for 1 minute.

Reduce the heat to low, cover the pot, and simmer until the prunes are falling apart, 25 to 30 minutes. Remove the lid and check to see how much liquid remains in the pot—you should have about 3 tablespoons. If you have more, cook a little longer until the liquid has reduced further. Remove the pan from the heat and stir in the sugar until incorporated.

Mash the prunes down with a potato masher, then, using an immersion blender, puree the prunes directly in the pot until smooth. Transfer to a 2-cup (480-milliliter) container and let cool completely before using. (You will have extra prune filling; it makes an excellent toast topping or addition to morning oatmeal. You can refrigerate the filling before making the hamantaschen; it'll be much easier to work with. Cover and refrigerate for a couple of hours, or transfer to an airtight container and refrigerate for up to 2 weeks, or freeze for up to 6 months.)

Make the dough: Place the flour, sugar, and salt in the bowl of a food processor and pulse until combined. Add the butter and cream cheese and pulse until the mixture resembles coarse crumbs.

Whisk together the egg and vanilla in a small bowl until combined. Add the egg mixture to the crumb mixture and pulse just until the dough begins to come together (do not overmix). Gather the dough into a ball, flatten it into a disk, and wrap it in plastic wrap. Refrigerate for at least 1 hour and up to 2 days.

Assemble and bake the hamantaschen: Position a rack in the center of the oven. Preheat the oven to 350°F (177°C).

Halve the dough; rewrap and refrigerate one piece and set the other on a cool, lightly floured surface. Knead the dough a couple of times to make it less crumbly. Roll out the dough to an ⅛-inch (3-millimeter) thickness and, using a 3-inch (7.5-centimeter) round cookie cutter, cut out as many rounds as possible. Using an offset spatula, transfer the rounds to a large baking sheet, leaving about ½ inch (1.5 centimeters) of space between them. Reroll the scraps and cut out a few more rounds. Put ¾ teaspoon of the prune filling in the center of each round and fold up the edges to form triangular cookies, pinching the corners together. Make sure some of the filling is exposed in the center. (You can use a wet finger to smooth out the filling. When pinching, be sure to be gentle but thorough; if you're too delicate with the pinching, the dough may open up during the baking.)

Bake the hamantaschen for about 20 minutes, until pale gold. Using an offset spatula, carefully lift a cookie or two to check the bottoms—they should be nicely browned. Set the baking sheet on a wire rack and let the hamantaschen cool for about 5 minutes, then transfer the cookies to the rack and let cool completely.

Repeat the process with the remaining dough. (If you have more than one baking sheet, you can assemble the second batch of cookies while the first batch bakes.)

The hamantaschen will keep in an airtight container at room temperature for up to 1 week.

Haminados

By Alana Newhouse

Look, I don't want to fight. If you must, you can use your Instant Pot for cholent, for chicken, for brisket, for *pkaila* . . . hell, you can use it to bake challah, too. But if you imagine for one minute that you can submerge a dozen eggs in some sleek gadget and come out with *huevos haminados*, you are misguided and in need of immediate instruction.

Huevos haminados—Sephardic slow-cooked eggs—cannot be properly made unless they are boiled in water filled with the detritus of your specific domestic life. My grandmother, whose family hailed from what is now Macedonia, made hers with Chock full o'Nuts coffee grinds and onion skins—she might also part with a Lipton tea bag, provided it had already been used 342 times (see page 274)— plus a few teaspoons of white vinegar. She brought the pot to a boil, during which streams of oniony coffee-grind water would drip down the sides and dry out, filling the air and sparking inquisitive stares from whatever Ashkenazi neighbors might be passing through her apartment. The pot was then set on low heat from Friday afternoon to Saturday midday, at which point what emerged were hard-boiled eggs with strikingly brown whites and greenish yolks. They tasted, for obvious reasons, like her home.

They are also eerily reminiscent of chicken, which makes sense once you understand the science at work. In his seminal work *On Food and Cooking*, none other than Harold McGee noted that the unique

→

flavor of these "Jewish eggs" was a consequence of the tiny amount of glucose sugar in the egg whites reacting with the albumen protein to create the flavors most frequently associated with browned foods.

Undoubtedly, some smart-ass will chime in to explain that what is described above is known as the Maillard reaction—which, he (it will be a he) will add, is precisely what you get with . . . the Instant Pot! I know this. What I am trying to tell you is that if you use it for huevos haminados, you will be depriving yourself and future generations of an important lesson—about life, home, and the magic that can be made out of your particular scraps.

HUEVOS HAMINADOS

Serves 6

6 large eggs, in their shells

2 tablespoons (about 10 grams) or more used coffee grinds, or whatever is left in your coffee machine from the morning

1 teaspoon vegetable oil

1 teaspoon distilled white vinegar

1 teaspoon salt

Skins from at least 2 large or 3 medium onions

1 to 3 used tea bags (optional)

Lemon wedges, for serving

Place the eggs, coffee grinds, vegetable oil, vinegar, salt, onion skins, and tea bags (if using) in a large pot and cover with cool water. Bring to a boil, then reduce the heat to maintain a gentle simmer. Cover and cook for at least 7 hours, but preferably overnight. (Check the pot occasionally—if enough water has evaporated that you can see the tops of the eggs, add more.)

Drain the eggs, rinse the shells, and serve with lemon wedges. The egg whites will be brown and the yolks green around the edges. And if you're lucky, the shells of at least one or two will have cracked in the process, thereby naturally giving the egg a marbled effect.

Hebrew National Hot Dogs

By Marc Tracy

My adherence to kashrut growing up was like that saying about whether you should button the buttons on a three-button suit: sometimes, always, never. Sometimes: milk with meat. Always: shellfish (I mean, I lived in Maryland). Never: pork. I still never eat pork, and with regard to bacon, I am confident I am missing out big-time. But I take pride in my allegiance to kosher hot dogs. They're better anyway.

Or so I've been told. I wouldn't know! Great hot dogs to me are delicious, juicy, without the dangerous smokiness I can only imagine the ones stuffed with pork have. My dad would get Second Avenue Deli dogs shipped, frozen, in bulk. When my parents and brother were away on Saturday afternoons for soccer games, I would stay at home with the George Foreman grill, squeezing the top down to etch those charred divots into the dogs, lightly splaying the buns on the grill near the end. Deli mustard. A Coke. I can't believe people eat them with ketchup.

My father told me about the Hebrew National ads: "We answer to a higher authority." A more concise statement of American Jewish assimilation I have not found. Our hot dogs are *better* than your hot dogs, because they must satisfy not only the demands of your profane laws of man but also our own sacred laws of God. Jewishness: It works. (Infant circumcision could take a page from this marketing strategy.) But, of course, the implied boast was unprovable, because those making it would never eat the other hot dogs. The slogan combined confidence in the reasoned superiority of one's faith with an orthodox commitment to that faith, regardless of reason. Many a group has refused to copy the American mainstream. But it takes something still known by its Yiddish name—chutzpah—to insist, "No, actually, you will copy *us*."

Herring

By Maira Kalman

Herring have been swimming around in large schools for thousands of years. Occasionally, a predator comes and eats them. And yet they survive. The ultimate Jewish experience. The ultimate Jewish fish.

Everyone in my family ate herring, except for me. They stank. They were oily and, in my opinion, hairy. Though I know a fish can't be hairy. But when my mother would eat a piece, I would see all these hairlike bones sticking out of her mouth. Herring were eaten with boiled potatoes. Sour cream. Thick slices of dark bread. The way they ate them for dinner in the little village of Lenin in Belarus. A family sitting around a table in a grubby shack, eating smelly fish. They were eaten with arguments and accusations. Or gentle love. With millions of questions being asked.

The family left Belarus. And came to Palestine. There was plenty of herring eating there. Then my parents moved us from what was by then Israel to Riverdale, in the Bronx. There were plenty of Jews there. No need to pine for that. Sunday was brunch day for everyone. My father would take me to buy the food for the brunch. Rugelach from Mother's Bake Shop. Knishes from Liebman's Deli. But most important was the trip to Daitch supermarket. There we bought bagels, cream cheese, tomatoes, nova. And the herring.

The deli counterman would plunge a big two-pronged fork into a pickled herring and, with a deft motion, place it on the wooden

$\longrightarrow$

cutting board and slice it into pieces. Then they were spilled into a container that was filled with cream and onions. The cream and onions were, to me, the only good part. We brought the herring home and had our own version of sitting around a table. Some arguments. Some silence. Some singing. A messy mix of inexplicable actions and emotions. With a certain amount of festive exuberance and cultural comfort. And so it went. And so it still goes.

Chekhov and the Herring.   M. Kalman

When Chekhov died, his body was sent to the funeral in a refrigerated train car full of herring. They accompanied the great writer to his end. The fish were innocently sitting in their boxes next to the big box of Chekhov. That is enough to make you like them. And now I actually do.

Honey

By Merissa Nathan Gerson

On Rosh Hashanah, we dip apples (page 19) in honey and eat honey cake to ensure a sweet new year. But honey's connection to Judaism goes beyond the table.

It's not a coincidence that we talk about "the birds and the bees" in reference to sex and mating. For centuries, religious groups have looked to the bees, in particular, to learn about channeling and bridling desire. Monastic groups often kept bees—cohesive mass producers—as reminders and teachers of how to redirect unused sexual energy.

Drone bees mate with the queen before splitting in half and dying, but all other honeybees are nonreproductive and work their whole lives, tending to the larvae, collecting pollen, protecting the queen, or performing any number of other highly specific jobs. Sexual energy that might otherwise be used for mating is proactively engaged in the production of honey and the maintenance of a well-ordered and tight-knit bee universe.

If we anthropomorphize the bees and make them Jewish bees, we can overlay their behaviors with the traditional Jewish laws of *niddah*. These are Jewish laws around sexual abstinence, and a call to infuse God and the divine into sexual engagement.

During Jewish periods of sexual abstinence, it is suggested this energy be used to perform acts of *tikkun olam*, study Torah, or

$\longrightarrow$

generally apply oneself toward the greater good of the Jewish collective. While bees produce honey, I like to think of Jewish laws around sex, when applied with care, as yielding something, too: a sweet substance that comes in the form of *tzedakah*, of building community, and making the world brighter through devotional practice.

HONEY CAKE

Makes two 8 by 4-inch (20 by 10-centimeter) loaves

⅔ cup (160 milliliters) neutral-flavored vegetable oil (such as sunflower, grapeseed, or avocado), plus more for greasing

3½ cups (435 grams) unbleached all-purpose flour

2 teaspoons baking soda

½ teaspoon kosher salt

⅔ cup (135 grams) sugar

2 teaspoons packed lemon zest

1 teaspoon ground cinnamon

½ teaspoon ground ginger

½ teaspoon ground cardamom

4 large eggs

1 cup (240 milliliters) honey

⅔ cup (160 milliliters) fresh orange juice

Position a rack in the center of the oven. Preheat the oven to 325°F (163°C). Grease two 8 by 4-inch (20 by 10-centimeter) loaf pans with oil, line them with parchment paper, and grease the parchment.

Whisk together the flour, baking soda, and salt in a large bowl until well combined.

Combine the sugar and lemon zest in a small bowl, rubbing them together with your fingers for about a minute, until the sugar is moistened with the zest and infused with its aroma. Add the cinnamon, ginger, and cardamom, stir well, and set aside.

In another large bowl, beat the eggs by hand using a whisk. Add the sugar mixture and beat for about 1 minute, until well combined. Add the oil, honey, and orange juice and whisk vigorously for about 2 minutes, until the mixture is light and uniform.

Sift the flour mixture over the wet ingredients and use a large spatula to thoroughly combine, scraping the sides and bottom of the bowl to make sure all the dry ingredients are incorporated.

Divide the batter between the prepared pans and smooth the tops. Bake for about 45 minutes, or until a toothpick inserted into the center comes out clean.

Let the cakes cool in the pans on a wire rack for 10 minutes. Remove the cakes from the pans and let cool completely.

The honey cake will stay fresh, wrapped in foil, at room temperature for up to 1 week or in the freezer for up to 2 months. It's best eaten on the third day—if you can wait that long—as it develops more flavor as it sits.

Horseradish

By Daphne Merkin

Made from horseradish root, sometimes beets, and little else, this fiery condiment offers more prepossessing foods a gentle kick in the pants. The perfect answer to the mildness of gefilte fish (page 114), *chrain*—as it's also called—comes in a more bitter white version as well as in a sweeter ruby-red one. It is sometimes used as an ingredient in cocktail sauce, but its real claim to fame is the heat it brings to Jewish delicacies. Let the WASPs have their Worcestershire; leave it to the Jews to turn suffering into a craving.

For those who are charmed by this condiment, as I am, it is possibly most gratifying eaten on its own, directly out of the jar.

BEET HORSERADISH

Makes 1½ cups (360 grams)

1 (6- to 8-inch/15- to 20-centimeter) piece fresh horseradish root, peeled and cut into 1-inch (2.5-centimeter) chunks (about 2 cups/170 grams)

1 medium beet, peeled and cut into 1-inch (2.5-centimeter) chunks (about 1 cup/60 grams)

⅓ cup (80 milliliters) distilled white vinegar, plus more to taste

2 tablespoons (30 milliliters) cold water, plus more as needed

1 teaspoon kosher salt, plus more to taste

¼ teaspoon sugar, plus more to taste

Using a food processor fitted with a shredding disk, grate the horseradish and beets in batches.

Transfer the shredded horseradish and beets to a bowl, protecting your face to avoid exposure to the pungent fumes. Remove the shredding disk from the food processor and affix the blade, then return the horseradish-beet mixture to the bowl of the food processor. Add the vinegar and water and process, stopping a few times to scrape down the sides of the bowl, until the mixture is finely minced and uniform, 3 to 4 minutes. If the mixture is too dry, add 1 teaspoon water and process for 1 minute more. Add the salt and sugar and process for 30 seconds more.

Taste and adjust the seasonings, adding more salt, vinegar, or sugar to achieve a sweet-sour flavor.

Transfer the horseradish to a jar with a tight-fitting lid, cover, and refrigerate. Serve with gefilte fish (page 116) and roasted or braised meats, such as brisket (page 54) or roast lamb shoulder (page 178).

The horseradish will keep in the refrigerator for 3 to 4 weeks.

Hummus

By Liel Leibovitz

Forget the heated arguments about the spread's true national origins. Forget the endless quibbles about who makes it best, or whether it should be smooth or chunky, or what, besides chickpeas, constitutes an acceptable topping (mushrooms may be on the menu, but they're never OK). Here's all you need to know about the state of hummus these days: It's the official dip of the National Football League. Like Waze or Gal Gadot, it's a cultural ambassador, an Israeli emissary here to insist that you love it no matter what, a garlic-kissed argument for the tanginess of the Jewish state.

HUMMUS
by Einat Admony

Makes about 5 cups (1.2 kilograms)

3 cups (600 grams) dried chickpeas

2½ teaspoons baking soda

2 large garlic cloves, finely chopped

⅓ cup (80 milliliters) tahini

3½ tablespoons (55 milliliters) fresh
  lemon juice

5 tablespoons (70 milliliters) olive oil

1½ teaspoons kosher salt

½ teaspoon ground cumin

⅛ teaspoon freshly ground black pepper

¼ teaspoon sweet Hungarian paprika, for
  garnish

Put the chickpeas and 1½ teaspoons of the baking soda in a large bowl. Add cold water to cover and leave to soak overnight.

Drain the chickpeas and transfer them to a large pot of water. Add the remaining 1 teaspoon baking soda and bring to a boil. Cook until the chickpeas are tender, 45 to 50 minutes, skimming off any shells that float to the surface.

Drain the chickpeas, reserving 1 cup (240 milliliters) of the cooking liquid, and let cool completely.

Combine the cooled chickpeas, garlic, reserved cooking liquid (see Note), tahini, lemon juice, 3 tablespoons (45 milliliters) of the olive oil, the salt, cumin, and pepper in the bowl of a food processor and process until smooth and creamy.

When ready to serve, spread the hummus on a plate or in a shallow bowl and garnish with the remaining 2 tablespoons (30 milliliters) olive oil and the paprika.

The hummus will keep in an airtight container in the refrigerator for up to 3 days.

NOTE: If you forget to reserve the cooking liquid, you can substitute 1 cup (240 milliliters) ice-cold water. But using the cooking liquid will give the hummus a richer, bolder flavor.

Hydrox

By Marjorie Ingall

When I was wee, Hydrox were kosher. Oreos were not. "This tastes exactly the same!" our mothers promised. (See also: *bokser*, page 46.)

If you went to public school, Hydrox in your lunch marked you as Other, same as a knockoff Izod or Kmart Famolares. They were yummy, sure, but they weren't the real thing. (Little did we know that Hydrox, which debuted in 1908, were actually the original, and Oreos, first sold in 1912, were the rip-off.) Oreos taunted us in their promise of real, goyish Americanness. My own expulsion from the Garden of Eden came via Oreo; at eight, I stuffed one into my sock and smuggled it into the backyard toolshed, so if God struck me with lightning, He wouldn't take out the whole house.

That Oreo didn't taste exactly the same as the Hydrox I had come to know, but it was pretty close. Even more of a surprise, I survived. The house survived. Hydrox did not. It was phased out in 1999 after the manufacturer was acquired by Keebler.

But in 2014, Hydrox was resurrected. Like . . . Jesus! It had awesome retro packaging, real sugar instead of high-fructose corn syrup, no hydrogenated oils, and a less sweet center. Marketed to fans of the original as well as label-reading millennial hipsters, it's now sold based on the idea that difference, small-scale-ness, history, and authenticity are cool. So Jewish.

HISTORY LESSON

In 1997, Oreos were certified kosher. Joe Regenstein, professor of food science and director of the Cornell Kosher and Halal Food Initiative, told students in a 2008 lecture how it all went down. "It was probably the most expensive conversion of a company from nonkosher to kosher," Regenstein said. The process took more than three years and millions of dollars. It involved rabbis climbing into the company's ovens (I know!). To meet the strictures of the Orthodox Union, the hundred or so ovens, each one about 300 feet (100 meters) long, had to be manually blow-torched inside on the highest heat.

Ironically, Nabisco, which makes Oreos, replaced the lard with trans fats, which are today considered demonic obesity-engendering child-killers but in the '90s were considered healthy, at least compared to animal fats. Eliminating the lard was a way to woo new cookie fans, Jewish and non.

Marjorie Ingall

Jacob's Lentil Stew

By Gabriel Sanders

When we talk about Jacob and Esau, the specifics of the lentil soup that the patriarch sold to his twin aren't usually the point. The story's importance springs from the fact that Esau was rash enough to sell something as valuable as his birthright for something as ephemeral as a bowl of beans. The moral couldn't be more plain: Don't be a dolt. Don't be like Esau. But there is something lost in such a telling—specifically, the recipe for the "red stuff" at the heart of their rivalry. To have prompted Esau to trade so much for so little, it must have been well-near divine.

JACOB'S LENTIL STEW

Serves 4 to 6

2 tablespoons (30 milliliters) olive oil

1 medium yellow onion, diced

1 large carrot, diced

2 to 3 celery stalks, diced

1 teaspoon salt, plus more to taste

¼ teaspoon ground turmeric

1 garlic clove, chopped

2 cups (400 grams) dried red lentils

½ cup (100 grams) barley

1 bay leaf

¼ cup (7 grams) finely chopped fresh parsley

¼ cup (7 grams) finely chopped fresh cilantro

10 cups (2.4 liters) chicken or vegetable stock or water

Freshly ground black pepper

Juice of 1 lemon

Heat the olive oil in a large pot over medium heat. When the oil is shimmering, add the onion, carrot, and celery and cook until soft and fragrant but not turning color, about 8 minutes. Season with the salt, then add the turmeric and garlic. Cook until the garlic is fragrant, about 1 minute.

Add the lentils and barley to the pot, along with the bay leaf, parsley, and cilantro. Stir and cook for a minute, then add the stock and bring to a boil. Reduce the heat to maintain a simmer and cook for 50 minutes, or until the flavors are melded and the vegetables tender.

Taste and season with salt and pepper. Add lemon juice just before serving.

Kasha Varnishkes

By Mitchell Davis

My husband is a palliative care doctor who helps people with serious illnesses make critical decisions, often at the end of their lives. Several years ago, I told him he had better learn how to make my family's *kasha varnishkes* because they would be among my final requests. A combination of toasted buckwheat groats, mushrooms and onions sautéed—or, rather, steeped—in copious amounts of butter, and fresh egg noodles cooked separately and mixed together in roughly equal proportions is about as much of a recipe as we've ever used.

I like to pack the resulting kasha varnishkes in a casserole, baste it with broth to keep it moist, and bake until browned before serving alongside brisket (page 52) or roast chicken (page 71)—perfect to soak up the pan juices. The butter is not exactly traditional, nor is it kosher, of course, if the kasha varnishkes is (or should it be "are"?) served alongside meat. But the butter is the secret to my family's recipe, which I have seen turn kasha haters into lovers in one bite—a mitzvah in the face of gastro-anti-Semitism, if you ask me. In a kashrut pinch, you can substitute freshly rendered chicken schmaltz (page 236) or extra-virgin olive oil for the butter, but the result will be less moreish.

Kasha was the staple grain of peasants in and around the Pale, and for many it still tastes of poverty. For me, it tastes of riches.

(Maybe it's all the butter?) While writing my Jewish cookbook, *The Mensch Chef*, I tried researching the origins of the dish and its name. Despite several oft-repeated theories, Yiddish scholars at YIVO cannot confirm the root of the word *varnishkes*. Their etymologists do not support the popular explanation that it's derived from the word *vareniki*—the Russian equivalent of the Polish *pierogi*—and that it had something to do with scraps of leftover dumpling wrapper dough tossed into the kasha pot. From a frugal cook's perspective, it's a nice story, even if apocryphal. No matter. Kasha varnishkes is delicious in the singular and in the plural.

KASHA VARNISHKES

Serves 8

FOR THE KASHA

2 cups (480 milliliters) boiling water, stock, or chicken soup

2 tablespoons (30 grams) unsalted butter (optional)

1 teaspoon kosher salt

1 cup (205 grams) uncooked buckwheat groats

1 large egg or 2 large egg whites, lightly beaten

¼ teaspoon freshly ground black pepper

FOR THE MUSHROOMS AND ONIONS

4 ounces (1 stick/110 grams) unsalted butter, or ½ cup mixed peanut oil and melted chicken schmaltz (page 238)

2 large yellow onions, chopped

¾ pound (340 grams) mushrooms, such as button, portobello, romano, or a combination, cleaned and finely chopped

2 teaspoons kosher salt

Freshly ground black pepper

8 ounces (227 grams) bow-tie pasta

Kosher salt and freshly ground black pepper

½ to 1 cup (120 to 240 milliliters) vegetable, chicken, or beef stock, if reheating in the oven

Make the kasha: Combine the water, butter (if using), and salt in a small saucepan and bring to a boil.

Meanwhile, place the buckwheat in a wide saucepan, add the egg or egg whites, and stir to combine. The buckwheat will clump together, but don't worry about it. Set the pan over medium-high heat and cook, stirring continuously, until the clumps of buckwheat break apart into individual grains and start to give off a distinct nutty aroma, 5 to 7 minutes.

Pour in the hot liquid, then add the pepper. Reduce the heat to low, cover, and simmer until all the liquid has been absorbed and the kasha has plumped, 25 to 30 minutes. Remove from the heat and fluff with a fork. Set aside.

Make the mushrooms and onions: Melt the butter in a large saucepan or skillet over medium heat until warm. Add the onions and cook, stirring now and again, until translucent, 7 to 8 minutes. Add the mushrooms, salt, and pepper to taste and cook, stirring often, until the mushrooms have given off most of their water and the mushrooms and onions are soft, about 10 minutes. Taste and adjust the seasonings, if necessary. Transfer the mushroom-onion mixture to a large bowl and add the kasha.

Meanwhile, bring a large pot of salted water to a boil. Cook the pasta until al dente according to the instructions on the package. Drain and transfer to the bowl with the kasha and mushroom-onion mixture. Toss until everything is combined, then taste and adjust the seasonings, if needed.

Eat the kasha varnishkes as is, heat them up in a pot on the stove, or make them in the morning and reheat them in the oven before dinner. To reheat, preheat the oven to 325°F (163°C). Transfer the kasha varnishkes to a 2- or 3-quart (2- or 3-liter) baking dish. Pour over about half the stock. Cover with aluminum foil and bake for about 25 minutes. Remove the foil; if the mixture looks dry, pour another ½ cup (120 milliliters) stock over it. Increase the oven temperature to 375°F (190°C). Bake for 15 to 20 minutes more, until the noodles on top begin to brown. Remove from the oven and serve.

Kichel

By Wayne Hoffman

A cross between a bow tie and a fossil, *kichel* doesn't seem to have much to recommend it. Lacking the sweet icing of a black-and-white (page 38), the joyous colors of a rainbow cookie, or the fruity lushness of hamantaschen (page 125), kichel is nonetheless the quintessential Jewish cookie: It has been gracing synagogues' kiddush tables (see page 155) after Shabbat services as far back as anyone can remember, widely ignored by even the hungriest of cookie-loving children. It is entirely possible that only a dozen of these cookies have ever existed, and that these same dozen have been there all along, put out week after week. Kichel is dry and brittle, filled with air; how would anyone know if it was stale?

And yet. Something magical happens to Jews when they turn forty. Kichel suddenly becomes delicious. The faint whisper of sugar, the way it crumbles when you bite it, its legendary dryness practically crying out to be dunked in a cup of coffee—or, better yet, a *glezele tey* (glass of tea).

What was once the butt of our youthful Shabbat jokes has become the best reason to come to synagogue. Let the children laugh; let the grown-ups eat kichel.

HISTORY LESSON

A century ago, a kiddush in one traditional Ashkenazi synagogue more or less resembled any other, centering around three unchangeable foods: pickled herring, kichel, and schnapps or whiskey. This humble and decidedly odd trifecta was, for years, synonymous with kiddush, the breakfast and social hour that follows Saturday-morning services.

In early twentieth-century America, Kiddush with a capital "K" (the blessing) gave rise to kiddush with a lowercase "k" (the social hour). Community leaders began to understand the importance of the synagogue as a place for congregants to rest and form relationships—especially for hardworking immigrants in a new and unfamiliar country.

From a gastro-sociological level, the development of kiddush makes perfect sense: Whenever Jews and socializing meet, a little nosh is likely to follow. But the specific nosh that emerged (herring, kichel, and schnapps) was no accident. "Early twentieth-century synagogues rarely had kitchens, let alone iceboxes or refrigeration," explained Gil Marks, author of the *Encyclopedia of Jewish Food*. So foods that traveled well and kept for long periods of time, like pickled fish, were ideal.

Because Kiddush is supposed to be said in association with a meal, that nosh also had to be substantial. Hence the kichel, an egg cookie sprinkled with sugar that, like other cookies, cakes, and other nonbread grain foods, requires one to say a *mezonot* blessing, bumping up its status to a near-meal. In a move that might horrify some contemporary taste buds, kiddush-goers would top the kichel with a juicy bite of fish and eat them together as a sweet, briny sandwich. And then there was the schnapps. Schnapps and whiskey were brought over from Eastern Europe, where they were considered *chamar medina*, or suitable ritual substitutes for wine. Never mind the whole issue about drinking early in the day; these drinks tasted like home.

Starting in the 1950s, though, things began to change. As Jewish communities acculturated, spread out, and climbed the social ladder, the synagogue kiddush followed suit, becoming increasingly elaborate. People's tastes changed, too. "By the time the baby boomers came around, chocolate chip cookies were common, even in kosher bakeries," said Marks. "Compare that to kichel and you're going for the chocolate chip!"

Leah Koenig

$\longrightarrow$

KICHEL

Makes about 36 cookies

1 large egg

6 egg yolks

¼ cup (60 milliliters) vegetable oil or other neutral flavored oil

1 teaspoon pure vanilla extract

2 cups (250 grams) unbleached all-purpose flour, plus more for rolling and shaping cookies

¾ cup (150 grams) natural cane sugar, such as Wholesome

¼ teaspoon salt

Stir together the egg, egg yolks, vegetable oil, and vanilla in a bowl. Set aside.

In the bowl of a stand mixer fitted with the paddle attachment, combine the flour, ⅓ cup (65 grams) of the sugar, and the salt. Pour in the egg mixture and mix on medium-low to medium speed, scraping down the bowl every once in a while, until the dough is shiny and stretchy, about 5 minutes.

Gather the dough into a ball and set aside. Wipe out the mixer bowl and sprinkle the inside with a bit of flour. Return the dough to the bowl, cover with a clean kitchen towel, and allow it to rest for 20 minutes to hydrate the flour.

Position the racks in the upper and lower thirds of the oven. Preheat the oven to 350°F (177°C). Line two baking sheets with parchment or silicone baking mats.

Halve the dough and set one half on a lightly floured work surface (keep the other covered with the towel). Roll out the dough, turning and flipping it and squaring up the sides so you have a rectangle about ¼ inch (6 millimeters) thick.

Lift the dough and sprinkle half of the remaining sugar underneath it. Sprinkle the rest of the sugar on top of the dough.

Cut the dough into rectangles about 1 by 2½ inches (2.5 by 6.5 centimeters). Space the rectangles 1 inch (2.5 centimeters) apart on the prepared baking sheets.

Turn one end of a rectangle over 180 degrees, twisting at the middle of the rectangle so that the dough now resembles a bow. Flatten it just slightly at the twist point to help prevent it from untwisting while baking. Repeat with the remaining dough.

Bake for 20 minutes, then reduce the oven temperature to 300°F (148°C) and bake until golden, 10 to 15 minutes more. Let cool completely on the baking sheets.

The kichel will keep in an airtight container at room temperature for up to 1 month.

Kiddush Cookies

By Alana Newhouse

"Those cookies were the beginning of the end of it all," he said to me. The young rabbi had invited me to speak to the machers of the synagogue he now led. But the community he most wanted to tell me about was the one in which he was raised, the one in Pennsylvania that was no more.

Cause of death: kiddush cookies.

Anyone who's frequented an American synagogue in the past half century knows what I mean—which is something of a miracle, since the list of touchstones still shared by the disparate strands of American Judaism numbers . . . I'll be generous and say it's in the single digits. But the cookies served after Saturday-morning services—a motley crew of sweet, pasty mounds, dabbed with chocolate or rainbow sprinkles and engineered to make you desperately need the grape juice on which a blessing had just been bestowed—are among them.

Anyway, back to my young rabbi and the story of his hometown. As it turns out, his mother was among a cohort of women tasked, for nearly two decades, with baking the cookies that would be served each Shabbat in their synagogue. That is, until the year the board hired an outside consulting firm to determine where and how it could cut costs. In what will come as no surprise to anyone who's ever worked with a consulting firm or seen an episode of *The Office*, the first line item in the suggested changes was "pastries." Cookies could be bought much cheaper, the firm noted, at a local supermarket.

What these geniuses didn't comprehend was the one-two punch they were issuing to the gut of lived experience. In one fell swoop, the primary Jewish institution in town transmitted a dual message: To the women who had put their time and affection into baking these cookies, week in and week out, for nearly a quarter century, it told them that their commitment to Jewishness and their community was dispensable; to everyone else, it asserted the primacy of money as the only truly important marker of engagement in Jewish life. A decade and a half later, the shul—once a vibrant hub of American Jewish non-Orthodox success—was all but dead.

So you can sit there and rail against secularism or BDS or intermarriage or whatever other threat you imagine is decimating American Judaism, but from now on you can't say someone didn't school you in the real truth.

I just want to say two words to you. Just two words: *kiddush cookies*.

KIDDUSH COOKIES

Makes 36 cookies

2 cups (250 grams) unbleached all-purpose flour

¾ teaspoon kosher salt

1 teaspoon baking powder

1 cup (2 sticks/225 grams) unsalted butter, at room temperature

⅔ cup (135 grams) sugar

2 large egg yolks

1½ teaspoons pure vanilla extract

¼ teaspoon almond extract

Rainbow sprinkles

6 ounces (170 grams) chocolate chips or chopped chocolate

Preheat the oven to 400°F (204°C).

Combine the flour, salt, and baking powder in a medium bowl and set aside.

In the bowl of a stand mixer fitted with the paddle attachment, beat the butter and sugar on medium-high speed for 3 to 4 minutes, until light and fluffy. Reduce the speed to medium and add the egg yolks one at a time, mixing well after each addition. Mix in the vanilla and almond extract. Reduce the speed to low and add the flour mixture. Mix to combine, increasing the speed of the mixer to medium once most of the flour mixture has been incorporated and periodically scraping down the sides of the bowl with a rubber spatula.

Transfer the dough to a spritz cookie press and pipe cookies out onto an ungreased, unlined cookie sheet, using two squeezes of the cookie press trigger per cookie and spacing the cookies 1 inch (2.5 centimeters) apart. Sprinkle with rainbow sprinkles or leave them plain so you can dip them in chocolate after they're baked (or do a mix of both).

Bake until lightly browned around the edges, 8 to 10 minutes. Let cool slightly on the pan for 1 to 2 minutes, then use an offset spatula to carefully transfer the cookies to a wire rack and let cool completely.

To dip in chocolate, melt the chocolate in a heatproof bowl set over a saucepan of simmering water (the bottom of the bowl should not touch the water), or microwave the chocolate in 30-second increments, stirring after each, until it has melted. Dip the cookies halfway into the melted chocolate, scrape off any excess chocolate from the bottom, and place on a plate. Top with sprinkles, if desired. Let the chocolate harden.

The cookies will keep in an airtight container at room temperature for up to 5 days.

Kishke

By Yair Rosenberg

Like many Jewish foods, from gefilte fish to cholent, kishke is the sort of thing that you'd never even think of consuming if you weren't raised eating it. But for those who were, the Eastern European combination of intestines and grain proves both utterly irresistible and undeniably deleterious to their health. Aside from being delicious, though, kishke also has the distinction of being the most influential Jewish food in American politics, and the only one ever elevated to a political litmus test. Did President Obama possess a deep affinity for Israel in his kishkes? The jury is still out on this pressing matter of presidential proctology, but Google returns 33,000 results for "Obama kishkes," with everyone from Jeffrey Goldberg to Debbie Wasserman Schultz weighing in on the question.

THE "STUFF" OF LIFE

When Juliet asked, "What's in a name?" she was not likely stuffing meat and meal into animal parts, but if she were, she'd soon get a useful lesson in Jewish food taxonomy. For those of us who are fond of the sweet inner parts, three names loom large: kishke, *derma*, and *helzl*.

What are the differences? The first and the second are largely interchangeable: Take a cow's intestines, stuff it with some fine schmaltz (page 236), some flour (or matzo meal, if it's that time of year), and some spices, and you've got yourself a kishke. The word is Yiddish for "intestines," but if you prefer a more Teutonic twist, you can also call it *derma*, as *Darm* is the German word for the exact same thing.

Helzl, on the other hand, stands alone: The casing here is a chicken's neck, which is then stuffed with schmaltz, chopped-up gizzards or hearts, and some fried onions.

If you're looking for culinary insights into which Jews eat which of the above and when, don't bother: All are ubiquitous, and all common across the board. Iraqi Jews, for example, know *helzl* as *tebit*, which also includes rice and herbs. Stuff skin with good stuff, and we'll eat it. A kishke by any other name will still taste as sweet.

Kosher Salt

By Lior Lev Sercarz

I wouldn't be surprised if most people who use kosher salt have no idea that it was created to soak up the blood in meat, purify the meat, and make it permissible to eat. But that's OK. It shows just how much our religion has affected our cuisine, and I like that.

In fact, I can't think of any other spice that has religious observance attached to it in this way. The idea of salt is very important to Judaism: It's sprinkled on challah during Shabbat to remind us of our covenant with God. When diluted in water, it stands in for the tears of slaves at the Passover Seder. And where would our appetizing shops and delis be without it? Salt is an ingredient that you can find in every Jewish kitchen in any culture, country, or place.

Perhaps it's also the reason we Jews have always been . . . a little salty.

THE KEY TO KASHERING

A kosher animal, once properly slaughtered, is not kosher until it has been salted and its blood drained. This goes back to the Bible (Leviticus 17:12), and how to best remove animal blood is debated in the earliest codes of Jewish law. For much of Jewish history, this task fell to the Jewish housewife, or whoever was preparing the meat at home, but today is usually done before the meat is bought. The salting takes place after the meat is otherwise prepared—defeathered for chickens or deveined for larger animals like cows and goats—and is one reason some people say kosher meat does not need to be brined (cooks, like rabbis, disagree on this point).

This whole process should take place within 72 hours after the animal is slaughtered. It takes roughly 2 to 3 hours. First rinse off any visible blood on the surface and remove any congealed blood or clots. Submerge the meat in water and soak for 30 minutes. (There are varying opinions as to why the meat is soaked, but many agree that it softens it so the salt will be more effective in penetrating its surface.) Remove the meat from the water and shake off excess water so the meat is damp but not soaking wet. Now salt the meat, using a coarse salt that has sufficiently large crystals so it won't be absorbed by the meat—this is where "kosher salt" (which was first marketed under the more appropriate name "koshering salt" before being shortened in the 1950s) comes in. Sea salt would also work, as long as the crystals are small enough that they can stick to the meat.

Some say the meat should be completely covered and packed in salt, while others say it need only be salted enough as to be inedible until rinsed. But basically, all agree it should be salted very well and all over.

Hang the salted meat or place it on a board in such a way that the blood can drain out freely and let drain for at least 1 hour. Any open cavity should be salted internally and placed downward. There should be sufficient space for the blood to drain out of the meat without pooling around it. Once drained, rinse the meat three times. This is to remove the salt so the meat becomes edible, but also because the salt is now full of forbidden blood. (The salt should not be rinsed onto utensils used for eating.) The first rinse should be under running water, and the meat should be rubbed and cleaned thoroughly. The second and third rinses can be done under running water, or the meat can be soaked twice in a basin of fresh water (prod and turn the meat over to properly rinse). Once rinsed, the meat is kashered and ready to be cooked.

Shira Telushkin

Kosher Sushi

By Yair Rosenberg

The Bible famously forbids observant Jews from eating any fish that lacks either fins or scales. That's why you'll never see shrimp, swordfish, or crab at your local kosher joint. Aside from this, however, kosher sushi is largely the same as regular sushi, except for the fact that it frequently appears in restaurants that have no business selling it—like delis and pizza shops—thus outing them as Jewish. Indeed, the superfluous sushi menu has become a staple of kosher establishments over the past decade. This proliferation has gotten so out of hand, with hundreds of kosher sushi bars in New York City alone, that the *New York Times* devoted an entire, somewhat incredulous, article to the subject. "I can tell you the when and the what," Rabbi Moshe Elefant of the Orthodox Union's kosher division told the paper of record, "but not the why."

Kreplach

By Gabriel Sanders

If the matzo ball (page 195) is the common man of Jewish soup dumplings—doughy, resolute, and ready to serve—the kreplach is the aristocrat: shapely, well-tailored, and with untold riches squirreled away in hidden pockets. Traditionally eaten around the High Holidays, kreplach—along with other stuffed foods—assumes a special significance during Sukkot and its later days, when it is believed that the divine decree inscribed on Rosh Hashanah and sealed on Yom Kippur is delivered up to heaven. Kreplach here becomes more than just a food. It is a kind of prayer.

→

KREPLACH

FOR THE DOUGH

3 cups (384 grams) unbleached all-purpose flour

1 teaspoon salt

3 large eggs, lightly beaten

¼ cup (60 milliliters) cold water

FOR THE MEAT FILLING

2 tablespoons (30 milliliters) grapeseed or other mild-flavored oil

1 medium yellow onion, finely chopped

¾ pound (340 grams) ground beef (short rib or 80% lean chuck)

1¼ teaspoons kosher salt

1 large egg yolk

3 tablespoons (11 grams) finely chopped fresh parsley

3 tablespoons (11 grams) finely chopped fresh chives

½ teaspoon freshly ground black pepper

FOR THE EGG WASH

1 large egg

1 teaspoon water

Pinch of salt

Make the dough: Sift the flour and salt into a large bowl. Create a well in the center of the flour.

Pour the eggs into the well. Start working the flour into the eggs, slowly, adding the water as you go. Knead the dough, taking it from shaggy to smooth and elastic, for about 15 minutes. (Alternatively, sift the flour and salt into the bowl of a stand mixer fitted with a dough hook, add the eggs, and begin to mix on medium-low. Add the water and mix until a shaggy dough forms. Mix for 8 minutes more, adding additional water, if needed, until the dough is elastic and smooth.)

Pull the dough together into a ball, place it in a clean bowl, cover with a damp towel, and refrigerate for 30 minutes.

Meanwhile, make the filling: Heat the oil in a large skillet over medium-low heat. Add the onion and cook, stirring regularly, until it browns and softens, 6 to 8 minutes.

Remove the onion from the pan, leaving any residual oil in the pan. Return the pan to medium heat and add the beef. Season with ½ teaspoon of the salt and cook, stirring frequently and breaking up the meat with a spoon as it cooks, until the beef is uniformly browned, 6 to 8 minutes. Return the onion to the pan, cook the beef with the onion for about a minute, then remove from the heat. Let cool.

Add the egg yolk, parsley, chives, the remaining ¾ teaspoon salt, and the pepper to the meat mixture and stir to combine.

To assemble, whisk together the egg wash ingredients in a small bowl. Set aside. Flour a baking sheet.

Cut the dough into quarters, setting one-quarter on a well-floured surface and leaving the rest covered with the towel. Roll the dough out to a roughly 14-inch (35-centimeter) square, about 1/16 inch (1.5 millimeters) thick. Cut the dough into 2½-inch (6-centimeter) squares.

Working with one square at a time, gently pull the dough along its edges, stretching it slightly. Place the dough in one hand and fill it with a scant ¾ teaspoon of the filling. Dip a finger of your free hand in the egg wash and run it along two adjacent sides of the square. Fold the dough in half over the filling, forming a triangle, with the two egg-washed sides against the two without egg wash. Pinch the edges together, making sure the filling isn't falling out and pushing it back in with an index finger if necessary.

Pick up the corners farthest from each other and wet one of the tips with egg wash. Overlap the corners and pinch them to seal. Place the kreplach on the prepared baking sheet. Repeat with the remaining dough and filling.

At this point, you can freeze the kreplach. To freeze them, place on a well-floured baking sheet and freeze until solid, then transfer to a freezer bag and freeze for up to 3 months.

To cook, bring a large pot of well-salted water or stock to a rapid boil. Drop in the kreplach and cook for 20 minutes. If cooking from frozen, boil 3 to 5 minutes longer. Serve as is or in chicken soup (page 76).

THREE TIMES THE CHARM

Kreplach are strictly an Ashkenazi—mainly Hasidic—specialty, appearing on the menu three times during the year: the day before Yom Kippur, Hoshana Rabbah, and Purim. On all three of these days, the theme of mercy versus justice comes into play. (Yom Kippur and Hoshana Rabbah, the seventh day of Sukkot, are days of divine judgment, and in metaphysical terms, the Purim story was a victory of mercy over justice.)

Though some people fashion triangular kreplach—seeing, in the three sides, the three patriarchs, three sections of the Jewish people (Kohanim, Levites, and Israelites), and three pilgrimage holidays—you can shape them any way you like. Unlike eating matzo and bitter herbs at Passover, eating kreplach is strictly a *minhag*, or custom—meaning that it's optional. But make these delicious dumplings once, and you'll opt in.

Carol Ungar

Kubbeh

By Gil Hovav

There are many things to say and write in favor of *kubbeh*, but there is no doubt that its best advantage is the fact that it gives Jerusalemites another reason to look down on Tel Avivians. There are no kubbeh restaurants in Tel Aviv. How do they live?

In Jerusalem, on the other hand, these are the jewels in our crown. These magic dumplings—the dough made from bulgur, semolina, potatoes, or rice, and stuffed with minced meat and herbs—are a grandma staple. They may be called kubbeh, kubbah, or kibbeh—it's all the same to Mama.

Kubbeh options are endless. You can go Iraqi and eat your kubbeh in beet soup, round, purple, and sweet, or go Kurdish and have it in a yellow sauce, sour and flat, or be an Arab and fry it, or be a snob and eat it stuffed only with *siska* (beef confit), or maybe go to the extreme and eat only *kubbeh hamo*—a giant version of the dish that was actually invented in the Mahane Yehuda Market.

Anyway, whatever you choose to eat, the important part is to say, "They don't have it in Tel Aviv. Of course they don't. How could they? Filling kubbeh so the dough does not tear requires craftsmanship that they can never achieve. It's all in Grandma's wrist." (And please don't tell anyone that we all cheat and fill our kubbeh the easy way: You roll tiny meat patties, freeze them, then cover with dough. This is a Jerusalemite secret.)

HISTORY LESSON

Sarit Agai is the current matriarch of Mordoch restaurant in Jerusalem's Mahane Yehuda Market; her husband, Itzhak, and his father founded Mordoch, a homey, paper-tablecloth type of place, thirty years ago. The first restaurant was Itzhak's grandfather's, back when the Mahane Yehuda shuk was the spiritual center of the city and a melting pot for Jews of the Muslim world. Kubbeh had been most associated with Iraqi and Kurdish Jews, but the Agais are themselves mutts: Iraqi, says Agai, and "the other half is seven generations here in Israel from the Old City of Jerusalem. And another part from Persia and another part from Iraq, a *blila* [miscegenation] from generation to generation." She herself is half Moroccan and half Spanioli, Sephardic in Jerusalem for many generations—some straight from Madrid in 1492, some via Turkey and Egypt.

That was typical of who was peopling the alleys of the shuk when, back in the '60s, "there was a communal oven where everyone knew whose bread was whose by the marks," says Agai. That's why they have stuffed cabbage (page 252) on the menu, and *shakshuka* (page 241) with fresh crushed tomatoes, and cigarim and mejadra and even goulash.

Most people come for the soups, especially the older Jerusalemites who have fewer and fewer people with whom to reminisce about the Old World, and the visiting South American children of Iraqi Jews. "There are people that come in for kubbeh and say that they want to cry, because their mother is dead," Agai says. Her own children work the kitchen and the tables.

By now, you can buy frozen kubbeh in the supermarket, but Mordoch is one of the few places that hasn't changed—the Agai family still makes everything by hand, same as thirty years ago, nothing frozen and scarcely anything even ground by machines. They buy their produce in the morning at the shuk. "Our kubbeh is immediate, it's here and now," says Agai. "There'll be new kubbeh in the morning."

Irin Carmon

→

KUBBEH HAMUSTA SOUP

Serves 6 to 8; makes about 36 dumplings

FOR THE DUMPLINGS

2 pounds 3 ounces (1 kilogram) finely ground semolina flour, plus more for rolling dumplings

5 to 6 tablespoons (75 to 90 milliliters) vegetable oil, plus more as needed

1¾ cups (420 milliliters) water, plus more if needed

2 large yellow onions, chopped

1 pound 1½ ounces (500 grams) ground beef

Kosher salt and freshly ground black pepper

4 garlic cloves, chopped

6 celery stalks, with leaves, finely chopped

FOR THE SOUP

6 celery stalks, with leaves, coarsely chopped

6 Swiss chard leaves (including white parts), thinly sliced

6 scallions, coarsely chopped

4 garlic cloves, minced

3 quarts plus 3 cups (1.75 liters) water

Kosher salt and freshly ground black pepper

⅓ cup (80 milliliters) fresh lemon juice, plus more to taste

2 tablespoons (30 milliliters) vegetable oil

3 medium zucchini, split lengthwise and sliced into ½-inch-thick (1.5 centimeter) half-moons

Lemon wedges, for serving

Make the dumplings: Mix the semolina and vegetable oil in a large bowl. While kneading, gradually add the water until a soft, homogenous, and easy-to-work-with dough forms. The dough should have the consistency of soft Play-Doh. If the dough seems too dry, add more water 1 tablespoon (15 milliliters) at a time until you achieve the desired consistency. Transfer the dough to a clean, lightly oiled bowl, cover, and let rest at room temperature for 30 minutes.

While the dough rests, coat the bottom of a pan with vegetable oil and heat the oil over medium heat. When the oil just begins to shimmer, add the onions and cook, stirring now and again, until browned, 20 to 30 minutes. Using a slotted spoon, transfer the onions to a large bowl and set aside. Add the ground beef to the pan, season with salt and pepper, and cook, stirring and mashing the meat with a fork, until dark brown and crumbly, about 10 minutes. Turn off the heat, transfer the meat to the bowl with the onions, and add the garlic and celery. Taste and season with salt and pepper, if needed.

Divide the dough into balls the size of an egg and flatten each ball to form a thin disk. Place 1 tablespoon (12 grams) of the filling in the center of each disk, close, and shape to form a ball. Gently flatten the balls to form thick disks, then gently roll the dumpling in semolina and set aside. Repeat until you are out of dough or filling, whichever comes first. Loosely cover the formed dumplings with a barely moist kitchen towel or plastic wrap and set aside until ready to cook.

Make the soup: Combine the celery, chard, scallions, garlic, water, and salt and pepper to taste in a large stockpot. Stir in the lemon juice and vegetable oil. Bring the soup to a boil over medium-high heat, reduce the heat to low, and simmer until the vegetables are tender, about 15 minutes.

Gently slide the dumplings into the soup and stir slowly. Add the zucchini and bring the soup back to a boil. Reduce the heat to medium so the soup is at a lively simmer and cook until the zucchini is tender, about 15 minutes.

Ladle the soup into bowls and serve hot with lemon wedges on the side.

Kugel

By Michael Solomonov

The kugel that you grew up with, with the cottage cheese and the noodles and the pineapple and sugar and raisins? I hate to break it to you, but that is a shitty representation of Jewish food. It's like spaghetti with meatballs on top and a side of bread—a European dish with American resources and terrible results.

Now, I can get behind a wild mushroom kugel served with a nice salad, or a cheese kugel with real vanilla and orange zest, baked up fluffy like a soufflé. At Zahav, we've made kugel like *fideos* with short, skinny noodles, thrown in leftover coffee-rubbed brisket, and served it in individual cast-iron crocks. In the end, a kugel rises or falls on who's making it—since it really is just a kind of casserole.

That said, Yerushalmi kugel, I'll confess, is the shit. It's dark and slow-roasted and full of black pepper, and each strand of pasta tastes like it's been caramelized. And I've heard that on the Friday before Purim, some Jews eat four kinds of kugel—apple, flour, noodle, and potato—since in Yiddish, the first letters of each flavor spell out the name Amalek, an enemy of the Jews, which is a cute tradition.

But still: No thanks. I'd rather have hamantaschen.

→

YERUSHALMI KUGEL

Serves 6 to 8

1 (12-ounce/340-gram) package thin egg
   noodles

1 cup (200 grams) sugar

⅓ cup (80 milliliters) vegetable oil

4 large eggs

1 teaspoon kosher salt

2 teaspoons freshly ground black pepper

Cook the noodles according to the package directions. Drain, transfer to a bowl, and set aside to cool.

Preheat the oven to 350°F (177°C).

Combine the sugar and vegetable oil in a small saucepan and heat over low heat, stirring to dissolve the sugar. Increase the heat to medium and cook, stirring occasionally, until the sugar turns a medium brown color, about 10 minutes. (The sugar might seem lumpy at first but will eventually dissolve. Don't expect it to become homogenous with the oil—you should see the sugar browning on the bottom and the oil covering it on top.)

Immediately pour the sugar and oil over the noodles and toss with tongs to distribute and separate any lumps (some will remain, which is fine). Let cool to room temperature.

Mix the eggs with the salt and pepper in a medium bowl, then add them to the noodle mixture. Toss together to distribute.

Transfer the mixture to a 9 by 13-inch (23 by 33-centimeter) baking pan. Cover the pan with aluminum foil and bake for 30 minutes. Remove the foil and bake for 30 minutes more, or until the kugel is browned on top and you can see crispy noodles, especially in the corners of the pan. Serve hot or warm.

Labda

By Darra Goldstein

Say "potato pancakes" and latkes come to mind, at least for Eastern European and American Jews. But not so for the Jews of the Republic of Georgia, descendants of one of the world's oldest Jewish communities, dating back some 2,600 years. Though the Jewish population plummeted when the Soviet Union collapsed, the beautiful synagogues survive, notably in the capital city of Tbilisi, the central Georgian city of Kutaisi, and the town of Oni in the mountainous province of Racha.

Racha's real fame derives from its potatoes, which are prized throughout Georgia. The local Jewish population turned them into *labda*, a distinctively Georgian riff on potato pancakes. Boiled potatoes are mashed and mixed with chopped walnuts—the hallmark of Georgian cuisine. Beaten eggs and minced parsley are stirred into the mass, which is then cooked in a large skillet to make a single dramatic pancake.

Labda joins two Jewish culinary cultures in a sumptuous union. The use of walnuts and the frittata-like presentation are typical of Persian cuisine and hearken back to Georgia's ancient Mizrahi traditions, while the Russian Ashkenazim brought a taste for potato pancakes to Georgia when they arrived in the nineteenth century.

$\longrightarrow$

Labda is traditionally served at Passover. It contains parsley and potatoes, either of which Ashkenazi Jews typically place on the Seder plate for the *karpas* that symbolizes spring. The pancake's lineage is both ancient and modern, as it assimilates the potatoes beloved of Ashkenazi Jews into the Eastern-inspired cooking of the Mizrahim who settled in Georgia thousands of years ago.

LABDA

Serves 8

1 pound (455 grams) potatoes, such as Yukon Gold

1 cup (120 grams) finely chopped walnuts

2 tablespoons (6 grams) finely chopped fresh parsley

1 teaspoon kosher salt, plus more as needed

Freshly ground black pepper

4 large eggs, beaten

2 tablespoons (30 grams) unsalted butter

2 tablespoons (30 milliliter) corn oil

Place the potatoes in a pot and add enough water to cover them by about 2 inches (5 centimeters). Bring the water to a boil over high heat. Cook the potatoes at a rapid boil until tender, about 20 minutes. Remove from the heat and drain. Transfer the potatoes to a large bowl and let sit until cool enough to handle, then peel and mash the potatoes until fairly smooth but with some small lumps remaining. Stir in the walnuts, parsley, salt, and pepper to taste. Taste and adjust the seasonings, if needed. Add the eggs and mix to thoroughly combine.

Melt 1 tablespoon (15 grams) of the butter with 1 tablespoon (15 milliliters) of the corn oil in a 10-inch (25-centimeter) skillet with sloping sides over medium heat. When the oil-butter mixture is hot, spoon the pancake batter into the pan, pressing down with a spatula to form an even cake. Cook until the bottom of the pancake is brown and crusty, 4 to 6 minutes. Slide the pancake onto a platter. Heat the remaining butter and oil in the skillet, then slide the pancake back into the skillet, uncooked-side down, and cook until brown on the bottom, about 4 minutes more. Slide the pancake onto a platter, cut into wedges, and serve immediately.

Lamb
(Not the Leg. And Definitely Not Roasted.)

By Ruth Reichl

Being a food editor is a great job—until the holidays roll around. They are the bane of every food editor's existence.

Consider the Seder. My first year as food editor of the *Los Angeles Times*, I called my sister-in-law in Tel Aviv to ask what she was planning to serve. She gamely sent me her recipes. These included an unusual charoset and a lovely leg of lamb roasted in mint. The photographs we took were beautiful, and I heaved a sigh of relief.

But I arrived the next morning to a flurry of irate phone calls. "What were you thinking?" readers wanted to know. How could I possibly print a recipe for a leg of lamb and call myself a Jew? As one caller told me, "As a mark of respect for the memory of the temple sacrifices, the eating of a whole roasted lamb on Passover is forbidden by the code of Jewish law called the Shulchan Aruch, which was first printed in Venice in 1565."

Jews who strictly interpret this rule will not eat roasted meat of any kind for their Seder. Others simply refrain from roasted lamb. More than one caller explained, rather testily, that lamb was fine so long as it wasn't roasted—but not if it was a leg.

"Why not?" I asked.

"Don't you know that the hindquarter of an animal is never kosher, because it contains the sciatic nerve?" (Well, actually, no, I didn't. But it turns out that while American butchers rarely bother with the fussy work of removing the sciatic nerve, Israeli butchers do; in Israel, hind legs are kosher.)

I found this entire Passover episode so chastening that the next year—and every year after that—I hired an expert in Jewish dietary law to go over the recipes. When I tried hiring him to review our Hanukkah recipes, he laughed uproariously. "Oh, Ruth," he said. "Hanukkah's not a real holiday. You can put anything you want on the menu."

He stopped for a minute and then conceded, "Well, probably not ham."

$\longrightarrow$

LAMB SHOULDER

Serves 6

FOR THE MARINADE

⅓ cup (80 milliliters) extra-virgin olive oil

1 large head garlic, separated into cloves (about 12)

Leaves from 5 sprigs thyme

5 sprigs flat-leaf parsley

Leaves from 2 sprigs rosemary

Leaves from 2 sprigs mint

1 tablespoon (15 grams) kosher salt

Finely grated zest of 1 lemon

Finely grated zest and juice of 1 orange

Freshly ground black pepper

FOR THE LAMB

1 (5-pound/2.3 kilogram) bone-in lamb shoulder, tied

2 cups (480 milliliters) dry white wine

1½ cups (360 milliliters) water

1 cup (130 grams) pitted prunes

4 sprigs thyme

1 sprig rosemary

Make the marinade: In a tall container, such as a 1-quart (1-liter) deli cup, combine the oil, garlic, thyme, parsley, rosemary, mint, salt, lemon zest, orange zest, orange juice, and pepper. Using an immersion blender, blend until the mixture is emulsified and the herbs are tiny green flecks.

Make the lamb: Pierce the lamb all over with a paring knife and transfer the meat to a gallon-size (4-liter) resealable plastic bag. Pour the marinade over the meat, squeeze the air out of the bag, and seal the bag. Refrigerate overnight or for up to 24 hours.

About 1 hour before roasting the lamb, remove the meat from the refrigerator and let it come to room temperature.

Position a rack in the lower third of the oven. Preheat the oven to 325°F (163°C).

Remove the lamb from the bag, shaking off excess marinade, and place it in a Dutch oven or a large roasting pan. Pour the wine and water around the lamb, scatter the prunes around, and add the thyme sprigs and rosemary. If using a Dutch oven, place a large piece of parchment paper on top of the pot and cover with the lid. (If using a roasting pan, cover with heavy-duty aluminum foil.)

Braise the lamb in the oven for about 3½ hours, or until tender but not falling off the bone. Increase the oven temperature to 350°F (177°C). Discard the parchment, cover again with the lid, and braise until the lamb is very tender and the top is browned, about 20 minutes more. Carefully transfer the lamb to a platter, reserving the braising liquid, and loosely cover with the foil. Let rest for about 10 minutes.

Pour off the fat from the braising liquid (you can try sticking the sauce in the freezer for 10 to 15 minutes so the fat starts to solidify to make the removal easier) and transfer the liquid to a gravy boat.

Remove and discard the strings from the lamb. Also remove the thyme and rosemary sprig. Using a carving knife, slice the meat and serve on a platter along with the sauce.

HISTORY LESSON

Of Judaism's 613 commandments, Maimonides teaches us, a whopping hundred have to do with sacrifices, which tells you everything you need to know about how central—and complicated—the practice truly was in the days of the Temple. Back then, there was a sacrifice for nearly every occasion: a sacrifice to atone for sin and a sacrifice to sanctify the peace, a sacrifice for Passover and a sacrifice to celebrate the firstborn male, a sacrifice required and a sacrifice volunteered. Each of these categories had their own specific rules, with the animal's blood poured on different parts of the altar according to the occasion and with its meat consumed either by the priests alone or by the public as well. Usually, though, the animal's blood was let into a special receptacle and then carried by the priest to the altar and ritualistically poured. Then the innards would be burned, the meat salted and roasted, the blessings recited, and the offering eaten and enjoyed.

When the Temple was destroyed and Judaism ceased being a sacrifice-based religion, a spiritual crisis ensued. A Midrash, or ancient commentary on the Torah, from around that period tells us of the famous Yohanan ben Zakkai, who was walking with his disciple, Rabbi Yehoshua, near Jerusalem when the latter looked at the Temple's ruins and lamented that Jews no longer had a place to atone for their sins. "Be not grieved, my son," said Rabbi Yohanan. "There is another equally meritorious way of gaining ritual atonement, even though the Temple is destroyed. We can still gain ritual atonement through deeds of loving-kindness. For it is written, 'Loving-kindness I desire, not sacrifice.'"

Amen to that.

Leftovers

By Elissa Goldstein

Every Jewish family, regardless of ethnicity or nationality, has a history of hunger. It's why we're so anxious about not having enough—which is why we're now often left with *too* much. Our *simchas* and holidays are abundantly catered. Leftovers abound—and what we do with them matters.

The most remarkable thing about my mother is that for thirty years, she served the family nothing but leftovers. The original meal has never been found.

This is, of course, one of the greatest jokes about food, attributed to Calvin Trillin—a true observation of family and thrift, with a fundamentally Jewish kernel of feeling. You know it when you see it. His original, slightly clunkier anecdote has been smoothed by time and the internet into the quippy pearl we all know—proof of just how resonant it is.

Given Trillin's family background—Jewish, immigrant, Midwestern—it's no surprise that leftovers were often the main course in his childhood kitchen. But irony aside, his shtick taps into the real, fraught experience of food scarcity.

And not simply scarcity, but the terror of abundance. Here the Talmud provides guidance. The biblical commandment of *bal tashchit*—to never unnecessarily destroy that which could be used—is interpreted by the rabbis as an injunction against unnecessary waste, particularly relating to food and environmental resources. Every kosher part of an animal gets used in Jewish cuisine—see chopped liver (page 85), *eyerlekh* (page 106), and *gribenes* (page 120). Saturday's leftover challah becomes Sunday's French toast. We don't always live out this ideal, but we don't need pop-up waste restaurants to get the message: You don't throw out good food.

In my own family, these religious and historical factors have culminated in the practice of minimizing—storing leftovers in the fridge in the most compact, efficient way, all the better to consume them to completion over the following week. My favorite Waldorf chicken salad is my mother's, made on Monday from Friday-night leftovers. When my siblings and I were young, my father often wouldn't order his own meal in a restaurant—he'd wait for us to finish, then eat our leftovers. (I later discovered that other friends' parents, also the children of Holocaust survivors, did the same.)

Cleanliness might be next to godliness, but using up all the leftovers? Now you're approaching the incontrovertibly holy.

Lox

By Marcus Samuelsson

In 1944, my grandparents took in a twelve-year-old girl named Frieda Wasser, who had escaped from a concentration camp to Denmark and waited until winter to walk across the frozen water to southern Sweden. My grandparents did not have a lot of money, but taking in another child didn't change their personal economy, because they just stretched the food. They had things both cultures could relate to, like herring and lox. But the only way they could afford cured salmon was because they made it themselves. And to this day, I believe it was because of this experience that adopting me, a black kid from Ethiopia, didn't seem so far-fetched to my own parents in the '70s.

I was raised in Gothenburg, but in summertime we lived in the small fishing village my father was from. There you needed to know three things: how to swim, how to take care of your boat, and how to be skilled with all things fish. Lox comes from the essential need, in the days before refrigeration, to preserve foods safely. We prepared it with sugar and salt and dill, and if you cured it overnight, it meant that you would smoke it the next day. If you cured it for two nights, it became gravlax. In Sweden, *lax* just means "salmon."

Before I came to New York, I lived in Switzerland, Austria, and France, and I was around chefs who came from all over Europe.

A lot of them were young Jewish chefs. We talked about smoking culture and herring and lox more than anything, and each time it reminded me of home.

→

HOME-CURED GRAVLAX
by Susan Spungen

Serves 10 to 12

1 cup (240 grams) coarse salt

1 cup (200 grams) sugar

2 tablespoons (16 grams) coarsely cracked black peppercorns

1 tablespoon (5 grams) cracked coriander seeds

1 (2-pound/900-gram) skinless salmon fillet

1 bunch dill

Mix the coarse salt, sugar, peppercorns, and coriander in a medium bowl. Set aside.

Use a pair of needle-nose pliers to remove the small bones from the salmon (see Note).

Line a glass or ceramic baking dish with plastic wrap, leaving plenty of overhang, and sprinkle about half the salt mixture into the dish. Lay the salmon fillet on top and cover with the remaining salt mixture.

Very coarsely chop the dill and place it on top of the fish. Wrap tightly in the plastic wrap, then wrap in a second piece of plastic wrap.

Place in the refrigerator and set something heavy on top, such as a small cutting board topped with some heavy cans, to weigh it down. Cure for 2 to 3 days, turning the fish occasionally.

When ready to serve, unwrap the fish, and wipe off and discard the salt mixture. Slice the fish across the grain on an angle, as thinly as possible.

Serve with bagels or toasted bialys (page 36) and cream cheese (page 94), or as part of an appetizing platter (page 31).

NOTE: The small pin bones will look like a row of white dots running along the fatter side of the fillet (not the side with the belly flap) near the center line. Run your fingertip along the flesh against the direction of the bones so you can feel where they are, then grip them firmly with the needle-nose pliers and pull them out.

Macaroons

By Molly Yeh

Odds are good that if you are a Jew who grew up in America, you can remember one specific macaroon that made you realize one very important thing: Canned macaroons are bullshit. For my friend Jeff, it was a chocolate macaroon his neighbor made. For Leah, it was a macaroon she tried at a Havdalah potluck. For me? It was a rice pudding–flavored macaroon I ate while walking to the subway in East Harlem after a visit to the magical Danny Macaroons factory. Living in a country with modern conveniences like flaccid store-bought canned coconut macaroons seems to have produced two eras in the lives of many: the one that came before the life-changing macaroon, and the one that came after.

→

The latter era started to gain momentum around 2011, when suddenly everyone had become gluten-free. Bougie macaroons with crisp golden shells and gooey delicious innards were popping up at specialty stores and bakeries. The Jewish-food-blogging world was churning out carrot cake macaroons and matcha macaroons to Jews and gluten-free gentiles alike. And being able to make the distinction between the French macaron and the Jewish coconut macaroon was suddenly a skill required of every foodie (another thing everyone had become by 2011).

What the pedestrian foodie might not realize, however, is that the French macaron and the coconut macaroon are, in fact, cousins. They share an ancestor: an Italian cookie made of almonds, sugar, and egg whites, which won the hearts of Jews way back in the day because it could be eaten on Passover. After migrating to France in the sixteenth century, this cookie was eventually sandwichified and fancied up into the Parisian macaron we know today. Elsewhere, including in the States, coconut was subbed in for nuts to make a sturdier, more shelf-stable cookie. Franklin Baker, a flour miller in Philadelphia who became America's first large-scale shredded coconut producer in 1897, is largely responsible for this development. But in Sephardic traditions, macaroons made with almonds (or pistachios, or pine nuts) remain the norm.

No matter where you fall on your personal journey of macaroon discovery, whether you're pre-canned-macaroon epiphany or post, one thing is for sure: It's just not Passover without them.

MACAROONS

2 cups (240 grams) sweetened shredded coconut

2 large egg whites

¼ teaspoon kosher salt

2 tablespoons (25 grams) sugar

1½ teaspoons pure vanilla extract

Preheat the oven to 350°F (177°C). Line a baking sheet with parchment paper.

Process the coconut in the bowl of a food processor for about 2 minutes, until it is ground to a fine meal.

In the bowl of a stand mixer fitted with the whisk attachment, beat the egg whites and salt on high speed for 1 to 2 minutes, until soft peaks form. Gradually add the sugar and beat for 2 to 3 minutes more, until stiff peaks form. Beat in the vanilla. Gently fold in the coconut by hand with a rubber spatula.

Transfer the mixture to a large piping bag fitted with a ½-inch (1.5-centimeter) star tip. Pipe 1-inch (2.5-centimeter) macaroons onto the prepared baking sheet, spacing them 1 inch (2.5 centimeters) apart.

Bake until browned on the bottom and on the edges, 16 to 18 minutes.

Let cool on the pan for 5 minutes, then transfer to a wire rack to cool completely.

The macaroons will keep in an airtight container at room temperature for up to 3 days.

Malida

By Leah Koenig

From the Passover Seder plate to the apples and honey of Rosh Hashanah, food and symbolism are bound together in Jewish tradition. But India's Bene Israel Jews have brought edible ritual to a new level. The community, which maintains a special connection with the prophet Elijah, created a ceremony that echoes the deity offerings found in Hinduism. The focal point of the ceremony is *malida*, a sweet porridge made from flattened rice flakes called *poha*, which gets flavored with jaggery and cardamom pods and festively decorated with fresh fruit, flowers, dried dates, almonds, and shredded coconut. Bene Israel Jews hold malida ceremonies on auspicious occasions—births and brises, engagements, graduations, recovery from sickness, even housewarming parties—gathering together to pray and offering the platter of malida to Elijah in thanksgiving. After the ceremony, the malida is passed around for guests to nibble—spreading the good fortune via fork.

THE LEGEND OF ELIJAH ROCK

One hundred twenty kilometers south of Mumbai in a small coastal town called Alibaug, off a side road accessible only to locals who know where to look, sits Elijah Rock. Believed to be the spot where the biblical prophet Elijah ascended to heaven, leaving behind the markings of a chariot and hoof prints etched auspiciously into the mountainside, Elijah Rock is a sacred site for Bene Israel Jews. Members of the community make regular pilgrimages here, with each visit culminating in a *malida* ceremony. The local community, which goes back to the second century BCE, had as many as twenty thousand members in the mid-twentieth century. Today less than five thousand Bene Israel Jews remain in India.

→

MALIDA

Serves 4 to 6

3 cups (235 grams) poha (flattened rice; can be purchased at specialty grocers or online)

4 cups (1 liter) boiling water

½ cup (80 grams) chopped jaggery (can be found at specialty grocers or online)

½ cup (28 grams) dried unsweetened coconut flakes

½ teaspoon ground cardamom

¼ teaspoon kosher salt

4 tablespoons (36 grams) pistachios, coarsely chopped

1 persimmon

1 pear

3 dried apricots

2 dates

4 kumquats

1 tangerine

3 dried plums, such as Angelino plums

Handful of edible rose petals

Place the poha in a large bowl and pour over enough of the boiling water so the poha is completely submerged. Let soak until the poha is softened and has plumped a bit, about 1 minute, then drain in a colander, tossing gently to remove as much water as possible.

Return the poha to the bowl. Add the jaggery, stirring until it is thoroughly combined and mostly dissolved in the rice; you may have to use your fingers to break it up further—no piece should be bigger than a lentil. If some smaller pieces remain, that's OK. Add the coconut, cardamom, and salt and stir to combine.

To serve, spoon the rice mixture onto a platter and garnish with the pistachios. Arrange the persimmon, pear, apricots, dates, kumquats, tangerine, and dried plums around the perimeter of the rice and scatter with the rose petals.

Margarine

By Taffy Brodesser-Akner

A thing you have to admire about margarine is that it is like Jews themselves: great at assimilation. It can hide in plain sight, with only a vague Uncanny Valley aura about it that something's off—it's not as creamy, not as sumptuous-smelling, not as delicious as butter. But it does what it needs to do, which is restore dignity to both the kosher-keeping and lactose-intolerant among us.* The only problem is, aside from the several qualities I have already listed in just three lines of prose, the more you know about it, the grosser it becomes, its double carbons flipped in the service of its lies, allowing something that should just be oil to hold a fork in a death grip. If that's what it does to a fork, then it's not a terrible leap to wonder how it behaves in your aorta.

But what are you going to do? Serve fruit? Not when there's margarine, you're not. So stop thinking so much and just empty a vat into your next cake. Life will be shorter, but it will be sweeter. Or something.

---

* *If you are neither, stop reading and go buy yourself some butter; you're doing everything wrong.*

Matzo

By Alana Newhouse

Perceptive readers will note that in putting together this book, we did not rank the entries. This wasn't merely a matter of self-interest, though we admit that the thought of spending hours fighting with critics about whether chopped liver was treated dismissively struck us as too close to a dystopian *Seinfeld* episode for comfort. But the truer reason here is that these foods represent the experiences of different people, places, and times in Jewish history. The majesty, allure, joy, and terror of this story reside in its diversity and complexity.

And yet it is not outlandish to argue that only one food was present at the creation of the Jewish people, and it has miraculously managed to sustain that bond over millennia: matzo—our unleavened bread of affliction and redemption. This is the only entry that is receiving a numerical value, because on a list of foods judged for their Jewish significance, none is more important.

It might not be anybody's favorite dish—it's certainly not the most delicious!—but it's arguably the only food that we all somehow eat, no matter where we live or where our family came from. The old saying "two Jews, three synagogues" accurately captures our age-old love of disputation and drawing distinctions, which can be fruitful and necessary but, at times, absurdly destructive. We might also do well to occasionally remember the gifts and pleasures that have come—for thousands of years—from staying committed to what we have in common.

Matzo Balls

By Joan Nathan

Here is my considered judgment: No Jewish dish—not one—is as comforting or iconic as the matzo ball.

With neither the heat of spicy Szechuan dumplings nor the delicacy of Italian gnocchi, there is no ambrosia quite like matzo balls, floating in homemade chicken broth, when you are sick or celebrating a Jewish holiday.

Matzo balls began as the German *Knödel*, a bready dumpling. Jewish cooks in the Middle Ages first adapted the dumplings to add to Sabbath soups, using broken matzo with some kind of fat like chicken or beef marrow, eggs, onions, ginger, and nutmeg. As Jews moved eastward from Germanic lands to Poland and the Pale of Settlement in Russia, they brought *kneidlach* (Yiddish for *Knödel*) with them. In Lithuania, kneidlach were filled with special bonuses like cinnamon or meat for the Sabbath. Though kneidlach arrived in America under different guises, the B. Manischewitz Company started packaging ground matzo meal like bread crumbs and marketed the dumplings in a box as "feather balls Alsatian style" in their *Tempting Kosher Dishes* cookbook of 1933.

The term *matzo ball* itself was first used in English in 1902 in the section on Jewish food in *Mrs. Rorer's Cookbook*, and the name stuck. Today matzo balls come in all sizes and varieties; there are those the size of tennis balls and even bacon-wrapped matzo balls.

⟶

And, of course, there is the age-old discussion of "floaters" versus "sinkers." You can make floaters with the packaged mix by including baking powder—yes, baking powder—or by adding, as my mother-in-law did, soda water to the prepared mix. Today I make mine using matzo meal, spices like ginger and nutmeg, and fresh herbs like cilantro, dill, or parsley for flavor and color and cook them the way I like them—al dente. Now *that* is what I call a matzo ball!

MATZO BALL SOUP
by Joan Nathan

Makes 10 to 12 matzo balls; serves 6 to 8

FOR THE SOUP

1 (4-pound/1.8 kilogram) chicken

2 large yellow onions, unpeeled

4 parsnips

2 celery stalks, with leaves

6 medium carrots

6 tablespoons (20 grams) chopped fresh parsley

6 tablespoons (20 grams) dill sprigs

1 tablespoon (15 grams) kosher salt, plus more as needed

¼ teaspoon coarsely ground black pepper, plus more as needed

FOR THE MATZO BALLS

4 large eggs

¼ cup (60 milliliters) schmaltz (page 238) or vegetable oil

¼ cup (60 milliliters) chicken stock

1 cup (130 grams) matzo meal

¼ teaspoon ground nutmeg

½ teaspoon ground ginger

2 tablespoons (6 grams) finely chopped fresh parsley, dill, or cilantro

1 teaspoon kosher salt, plus more as needed

Coarsely ground black pepper

Make the soup: Put the chicken in a large pot and add enough water to cover by 2 inches (5 centimeters—about 4 quarts/4 liters). Bring the water to a boil, skimming off the gray scum that rises to the top. Reduce the heat to medium-low so the soup is at a gentle but visible simmer.

Add the onions, parsnips, celery, carrots, parsley, 4 tablespoons (13 grams) of the dill, and the salt and pepper. Cover the pot with the lid ajar and simmer for at least 1 hour and up to 2 hours. Taste and adjust the seasoning.

Turn off the heat, cover the pot, and let the soup cool to room temperature. Refrigerate for 2 to 3 hours or up to overnight so the soup solidifies to a gel-like consistency and the schmaltz (fat) rises to the top and solidifies. Skim off the schmaltz and reserve it for the matzo balls.

Make the matzo balls: In a large bowl, using a soupspoon, gently mix the eggs, schmaltz, stock, matzo meal, nutmeg, ginger, and parsley, dill, or cilantro. Season with salt and 2 to 3 grinds of the pepper. Cover and refrigerate until thoroughly chilled, at least 1 hour and up to overnight.

When ready to cook the matzo balls, bring a wide, deep pot of lightly salted water to a boil. With wet hands, take some of the mix and mold it into the size and shape of a golf ball. Gently drop it into the boiling water, repeating until all the mixture is used.

Cover the pan, reduce the heat to a lively simmer, and cook for about 20 minutes for al dente matzo balls, and closer to 45 minutes for lighter matzo balls. To test their readiness, remove one with a slotted spoon and cut in half—the matzo ball should be the same color and texture throughout.

Just before serving, strain the soup, setting aside the chicken for chicken salad. Discard the vegetables, and reheat the broth. Spoon a matzo ball into each bowl, pour soup over the matzo ball, and sprinkle with the remaining dill sprigs.

NOTE: Like many Jewish foods, matzo balls are polarizing. First, there's the size: Some prefer a boulder big enough to occupy most of the soup dish, while others like a ball small enough to fit two or three to a bowl. Then, there's the texture. The larger balls, usually leavened with baking powder or seltzer, err on the light and airy side, aka "floaters." The more petite kneidlach typically correspond to a dense, "sinker" consistency. This recipe, which balances heft and fluff, lands somewhere in between.

Matzo Brei

By David Samuels

The ingredients are as basic as they come: matzo, eggs, pepper, salt. But matzo brei, like every other good thing on the planet, is about the doing, and because it is Jewish, there is a particular way it needs to be done. The matzo needs to be broken over a colander, so you can save the precious fine-grained dust. Then gently wash the matzo fragments until they start to get soggy. Add the matzo dust along with the eggs, salt, and pepper, and a kind of alchemy happens. Fry it up in enough butter to float a battleship, until you have something that looks like the proverbial dog's breakfast, or worse. Add grade A Vermont maple syrup, and you have something undeniably delicious.

Matzo brei tells a story that starts out where I live and includes nearly the entire history of my people, with asides about copper, fire, belief in God, and so forth. Once those conditions are no longer binding, the food you eat tastes different. It's part of someone's nostalgia trip. Matzo brei is impervious to that kind of treatment, which is why, when they grow up, your children will make their matzo brei for their children.

Is this not the entirety of the agony and the ecstasy of a 3,500-year-old religion in one dish, with the addition of maple syrup neatly folding in nearly everything that will seem worth preserving, two thousand years hence, about the whole North American Jewish experience—namely, New England, where the Puritans created a safe haven for all faiths while teaching their children Hebrew at Harvard and Yale; and where the Boston Red Sox, who might also be the Brooklyn Dodgers, play baseball; and where Robert Lowell and Robert Frost wrote poems that could have been written in Russian, all of which is merely another way of expressing the gratitude of a hunted people for the nearly unbearable sweetness of life in this place. It is arguable that better maple syrup comes from Quebec, where Montreal is, and therefore, by extension, Toronto, and also Hollywood, which is secretly run by Canadians, some of whom eat matzo brei. So eat it, and smile. But only on Passover, or the spell will be broken and you may as well order a Big Mac at McDonald's for all I care.

→

MATZO BREI

Serves 4 to 6

5 sheets matzo, broken into 2-inch
   (5-centimeter) or bite-size pieces

4 large eggs

½ teaspoon kosher salt

¼ teaspoon freshly ground black pepper

2 tablespoons (30 grams) unsalted butter

Place the matzo in a large bowl and pour 3 cups (720 milliliters) water over the top, or enough so the matzo is completely submerged. Allow the matzo to soak for 1 minute, until it is soaked through but still holds its form, then drain in a colander. Press the matzo gently to squeeze out as much liquid as possible, then set aside.

Beat the eggs with the salt and pepper in a small bowl until the whites and yolks are fully blended, then set aside.

Melt the butter in a large skillet over medium heat. When it starts to foam, add the matzo, making sure to coat all of it with the butter. Fry the matzo, stirring occasionally so it cooks evenly, until it starts to turn golden and fragrant, about 3 minutes.

Add the eggs and scramble with the matzo until the mixture is cooked through but still fluffy and tender, about 1 minute. Remove from the heat and serve immediately, with sweet or savory toppings, such as jam, whitefish salad (page 277), leftover brisket (page 54), charoset (page 66), salsa and guacamole, or cinnamon sugar.

Mina de Matzo

By Leah Koenig

At the heart of all Jewish cooking lies culinary ingenuity—that is, finding creative ways to eat well, despite Jewish dietary restrictions. It is not surprising, then, that Sephardic Jews managed to adapt their passion for savory pastries—*burekas*, *boyos*, *pasteles*, and the like—for Passover. During the weeklong holiday, the phyllo and other doughs that typically encase these parcels and turnovers are verboten. Instead, Sephardic home cooks bake *mina de matzo*—pies made from softened matzo sheets that are layered, lasagna-style, with fillings like sautéed eggplant and spiced lamb, or cheese, spinach, and leeks. Sliced small, mina de matzo (which is sometimes called *megina*, depending on where it is made) can be served as part of a Passover mezze spread. Presented whole at the table, it also makes a stately and hearty main course—no *chametz* required.

→

MINA DE MATZO

Serves 6 to 8

1 large bunch Swiss chard, washed and stemmed

3 tablespoons (45 milliliters) extra-virgin olive oil, schmaltz (page 238), or duck fat

2 large yellow onions, finely chopped

4 garlic cloves, minced

Kosher salt and freshly ground black pepper

1½ pounds (680 grams) ground beef, turkey, or chicken

4 cups (960 milliliters) quality marinara sauce, such as Rao's

9 sheets matzo

1 large egg

Preheat the oven to 350°F (177°C).

Fill a large pot with 1 inch (2.5 centimeters) of water and place a steamer basket inside. Cover and bring the water to a boil over medium-high heat. Put the chard in the steamer basket, cover, and steam for about 5 minutes, until the chard is wilted. Remove from the heat and transfer the chard to a bowl to cool. When the chard is cool enough to handle, squeeze out excess moisture and finely chop.

Meanwhile, heat the olive oil in a medium skillet over medium heat. When the oil is shimmering, add the onions and cook, stirring now and again, until the onions are translucent but have not yet taken on color, about 4 minutes. Stir in the garlic and cook, stirring, until the onions begin to caramelize and the garlic is fragrant, about 5 minutes. Season with a generous pinch of salt and some pepper.

Add the ground meat and cook, stirring and breaking up the meat with a wooden spoon as it cooks, until the meat is no longer pink, about 8 minutes. Season with a pinch of salt and some pepper, then remove from the heat and set aside.

Spread a third of the marinara over the bottom of a 9 by 13-inch (23 by 33-centimeter) baking dish.

Fill a shallow dish (large enough to accommodate the matzo) with water. Dip 3 sheets of matzo in the water and let them soften, about 1 minute. (You don't want to soften the sheets too much or they will fall apart.) Shake the excess water off the softened matzo sheets and arrange them over the marinara in the baking dish, breaking the matzo as necessary to fit. Top with half the ground meat mixture, followed by about half the chopped chard. Repeat with another third of the marinara, 3 soaked matzo sheets, then the remaining meat mixture, the remaining chard, and the remaining marinara. Place the remaining 3 matzo sheets on top.

In a small bowl, beat the egg with 1 tablespoon water until combined. Generously brush the top layer of matzo with the egg wash. Set the egg wash aside.

Cover with aluminum foil and bake for about 45 minutes, or until cooked through. Remove the foil (set it aside—you may need it later to store the leftover mina de matzo). Brush the top of the mina de matzo with the remaining egg wash, return it to the oven, and bake, uncovered, until the top is golden and glossy, about 15 minutes more. Let stand for 5 minutes before cutting into pieces, as you would lasagna, and serving.

Mufleta

By Gabriel Stulman

The best part of Passover is when it's over.

When I was growing up, Passover was dominated by my mother's side of the family, extremely observant Sephardic Jews from Morocco. My mom believed Passover was a holiday absolutely worth staying home from school for, though mostly so we could help clean the house of *chametz*—she gave my siblings and me toothbrushes to get into the corners of the carpet. The Seder always started with my grandfather Joseph and his wife, Perla—the "Joseph" of my restaurant Joseph Leonard and the "Perla" of my old restaurant Perla Cafe. Everyone wore caftans and djellabas. Each passage of the Haggadah was read in Hebrew, with Sephardic rhythms and Moroccan songs. There was a break after every single passage for debate, which took place in several different languages.

We kept kosher, so I always brought my own lunch to school. But my brown-bag lunches that week were different. Even my Jewish friends couldn't believe it: "Your mom makes you eat matzo all week?" And let me tell you: Eating a peanut butter and jelly or turkey sandwich with matzo is a hot mess.

But finally, when the sun set on the last day of Passover, it was time for Mimouna—which meant it was time for fun. And not only because I was at that point very sick of matzo. My grandmother would come over, and she and my mom would make all these different Moroccan

$\longrightarrow$

pastries, filled with dates, prunes, and pistachios. But the highlight of Mimouna was always *mufleta*.

The best way to describe mufleta is as a thicker crepe or blintz. It's not quite as thick as naan or as bready as pita. It's a bit like a tortilla, except puffier. Think of Neapolitan pizza and the blackened, crisp, burnt part under the crust. The perfect mufleta is thirty seconds away from that pizza—right before it turns black.

My mom and my grandmother rolled out the dough, threw it in a cast-iron skillet, and cooked it until it blistered. They stacked the mufleta like pancakes and covered them with a big kitchen towel for later, when they'd be warm, spongy, and a little bit oily from all the butter. That was the secret: all the butter. (Every time you finish cooking one, you add butter, so that when you put the new dough in, it oils up the bottom half.)

And then there were the fillings. The most popular were apple and honey, of course—lavender-infused honey, chamomile-infused honey. Then you'd line the mufleta with apples or bananas. My mom made a chocolate spread similar to Nutella, and I'd spoon that in. And that was the meal. You would just eat sweets for an entire dinner.

I have all these great memories of just stuffing my face with mufleta, and they came rushing back to me last year. My wife and I were invited to eat at Per Se, and the pastry chef, Anna Bolz, wanted to do something to surprise us. She had James Lauer, the general manager at our restaurant Fairfax, get in touch with my sister for recommendations. My sister told James about mufleta. Anna looked it up online, studied the principles of the dish, and made an entire mufleta dessert course at Per Se. It was like that scene in *Ratatouille* when the critic takes the bite of ratatouille and gets zapped back to being a kid. That happened to me. I literally cried in the restaurant.

HISTORY LESSON

Items symbolizing luck are central to Mimouna, and the festive table is decorated with "an array of symbols that are basically variations on a theme," explains Israeli historian Yigal Bin-Nun. Some families display a whole fish—even alive, swimming in a bowl of water—on the Mimouna table as a sign of good fortune, and also because the holiday is said to fall on the day when God parted the Red Sea for the Israelites to cross to freedom. Foods are often served in numerical groupings, such as seven green pea pods dotting a plate of flour to symbolize fertility and renewal. In some homes, Hanukkah gelt–like gold coins are strewn across the table.

Though the festival's name is often thought to refer to the twelfth-century's Rabbi Maimon (the father of Maimonides), Bin-Nun has uncovered folkloristic songs and historic sources that link it to the rituals of the Gnawa, a Sufi sect in Morocco whose adherents pray yearly through songs, parades, and ecstatic dancing to the goddess of luck, Mimouna. Sure enough, Bin-Nun says, during Jewish Mimouna celebrations, "songs are sung in honor of 'Lady Luck.' One of them is '*Lala mimouna/mbarka masuda*,' which means 'Lady Mimouna/lucky and blessed.'" The Arabic word *mimoun* also means "luck" or "good fortune."

Today in Israel, Mimouna is considered more or less a national party, and Israelis will point to its celebration as an example of peaceful relations not only between Sephardim and Ashkenazim but also between Muslims and Jews. After all, the culinary traditions of the holiday originate with Arab and Berber families who lent flour and yeast to their Jewish neighbors following sundown after Passover. In return, Moroccan Jews are said to have either given them the remainder of their matzo or opened their homes and eaten their first baked goods together—a tradition still maintained with Moroccan Jews leaving their front doors open on Mimouna eve.

Lara Rabinovitch

→

MUFLETA
by Uri Scheft

Makes one 14-inch (35-centimeter) pan of mufleta (about 24 sheets)

1 cup plus 3 tablespoons (300 grams) cool room-temperature water

2 tablespoons (15 grams) fresh yeast, or 1 teaspoon (5 grams) active dry yeast

4¾ cups (500 grams) cake flour or white pastry flour, sifted, plus more for dusting

1 teaspoon sugar

½ teaspoon fine sea salt

3 to 4 cups (720 to 960 milliliters) neutral oil

Unsalted butter, at room temperature, for serving

Honey, for serving

Combine the water and yeast in the bowl of a stand mixer and whisk by hand until the yeast is mostly dissolved. Add the flour, sugar, and salt. Fit the dough hook on the mixer and mix on low speed until the dough comes together into a semismooth ball, about 2 minutes.

Transfer the dough to a lightly floured work surface. Stretch one corner of the dough out and fold it on top of the middle of the dough. Give the dough a quarter turn and repeat a few more times, until each corner has been stretched and folded twice to make a nicely shaped ball.

Lightly flour a large bowl and set the dough in the bowl; sprinkle the top with a little flour, cover the bowl with plastic wrap, and set aside at room temperature until the dough has nearly doubled in volume, about 30 minutes.

Pour 3 cups (720 milliliters) of the oil into a large bowl and set it aside. Lightly flour your work surface and set the dough on top. Pat and stretch the dough into an 8 by 12-inch (20 by 30-centimeter) rectangle that is as even as possible. Use a bench knife to divide the dough lengthwise into 4 equal strips, then into 6 strips crosswise, to yield 24 pieces. Holding one piece of dough in your hand, stretch one-quarter of the piece up and over onto the middle. Repeat with the other three sides to create a rough ball shape. Place the dough, seam-side down, on your work surface and repeat with the remaining pieces.

Wipe the excess flour from your work surface and cup your hand around a piece of dough. Push and pull the dough in a circular motion on the work surface until it is rounded into a tight ball with hardly a seam on the bottom. Drop the dough ball into the bowl of oil. Repeat with the remaining dough. Add more oil to the bowl as needed to make sure the dough balls are completely covered; you don't want them to dry out. Let them rest in the oil for 10 minutes.

Set a dough ball on your work surface. Using your hands, stretch and push it into a paper-thin sheet (try not to create holes, but if you get a few, it's OK). It should stretch very easily. Heat a large nonstick skillet over medium-high heat. Reduce the heat to medium and carefully lay the dough sheet in the pan. While the first piece of dough cooks, stretch another piece of dough. Once the dough in the skillet starts to turn golden brown, about 2 minutes, use a spatula to carefully flip it over. Lay the second sheet of stretched dough on top of the first in the skillet. Stretch your next piece of dough. When the bottom of the dough in the pan is golden brown, 2 to 3 minutes more, carefully flip the two layers over together and place the just-stretched piece on top of the stack. Repeat this process, stretching, flipping, and adding to the dough stack, until all the dough pieces are stacked in the skillet like a giant flatbread layer cake. While you work, adjust the heat as needed so the sheets don't get too dark. Remove the stack from the skillet and place it on a large plate.

Mufleta is best eaten hot. Serve with lots of butter and honey. To eat, peel away a layer of mufleta, add a smear of butter and a drizzle of honey, and roll it into a cylinder.

Olives

By Ben Wizner

Rabbi Meir asked: "What makes an olive a Jewish food?" [He was answered:] "Its use in any recipe or drink that is not a martini." And what is a martini? Rabbi Yehudah answered: "A martini is a glass that the goyim use to overcharge for schnapps." But Rabbi Simon said, in the name of Rabbi Yehoshua ben Levi: "A martini is four parts gin to one part vermouth." And what is a part? A part is the minimum amount required of something to fulfill an obligation. And what is that minimum amount? A *kezayit* [literally "like an olive"]. According to the sages, if one eats less than a *kezayit* of any foodstuff, one is excused from saying the preliminary blessing or the grace after meals. But does this ruling apply to the olive itself? Yes. Because an olive is the size of an olive, one may eat an olive without having to say the preliminary blessing or the grace after meals. And according to Rabban Gamliel, if one places a swizzle stick across two olives, that which passes beneath is not *chametz*.

It was told in a *baraita* that a goy walked into a bar and asked, "How many olives should be in a martini?" Rabbi Yosef bar Tender answered him, saying, "One, in tribute to the One Lord, but the olive must not be eaten." Rabbi Nachman bar Keep said, "One, in tribute to the One Lord, but it may be eaten only in an emergency [e.g., if you are too drunk to drive home and require some sustenance]." Rabbi Eliezer bar Back disagreed and said, "Two: one to eat before you drink, and one to eat after—as it is written: 'Prayer is helpful both before and after the judgment is sealed.'"

Pareve Chocolate

By Elissa Goldstein

In 2012, a calamity struck kosher-baking enthusiasts in the United States when the supermarket chain Trader Joe's changed the certification on its semisweet chocolate chips from pareve to dairy. After the news broke, consumers rushed into stores to stockpile the remaining pareve packets, bemoaning the dearth of good-quality, kosher-certified, affordable bittersweet chocolate. Of course, there are other pareve chocolate chips on the market, but the urgency highlighted how important dark chocolate is to Jewish cooking.

If you follow Jewish dietary laws, you can serve a chocolate dessert after a meat main only if it's dairy-free. And no one wants to endure a three-day yontef without chocolate. Imagine Passover without a flourless chocolate torte or matzo buttercrunch or chocolate mousse. (It's very upsetting, right?) There are many substitutes for butter and milk, but when a recipe calls for chocolate, you need . . . *chocolate*.

Jews played an important role in the European cacao trade in the seventeenth century, and they weren't trading milk chocolate, which was invented only in 1875. The truth is, bittersweet chocolate is the best kind there is. (Fight me. I dare you.) Dark chocolate is complex, not cloying, and pairs well with other ingredients. It can be serious or playful. It's even good for you! Is it a stretch to say that the higher the percentage of cacao, the Jewier the chocolate? I don't think so. In life, as in dessert, Jews know from bittersweet.

FLOURLESS CHOCOLATE CAKE

Adapted from a recipe by Alison Cayne

Makes one 9-inch (23-centimeter) cake or eight 6-ounce (175-milliliter) ramekins

¾ cup (1¾ sticks/192 grams) margarine, such as Earth Balance, or unsalted butter, plus more for greasing

8 ounces (227 grams) bittersweet chocolate (70% cacao or more), chopped

5 large eggs

¾ cup (150 grams) sugar

Fine sea salt

¼ cup (35 grams) almond meal (optional)

Preheat the oven to 375°F (190°C). Grease the sides of a 9-inch (23-centimeter) round cake pan and line the bottom with a round of parchment paper cut to fit. (Alternatively, grease eight 6-ounce/175-milliliter ramekins to make individual cakes.)

Melt the margarine in a small pot over medium heat, stirring occasionally. Remove from the heat and add the chocolate. Stir continuously until the chocolate has melted and the mixture is well combined. Set aside to cool.

In the bowl of a stand mixer fitted with the whisk attachment or in a large bowl using a handheld mixer, beat the eggs, sugar, and a pinch of salt on medium-high speed until pale yellow and doubled in volume, about 3 minutes.

Using a silicone spatula, fold the melted chocolate mixture into the whipped eggs in three additions so the chocolate doesn't sink to the bottom and the batter remains nicely aerated.

Fold in the almond meal (if using), then pour the batter into the prepared pan or divide it evenly among the prepared ramekins. If using a cake pan, set it on an even surface and give it a quick spin, which will cause the batter to climb up the sides of the pan and bake more evenly.

Bake until the top is set and dry to the touch, 20 to 25 minutes for a 9-inch (23-centimeter) cake or 10 to 15 minutes for ramekins.

Let cool in the pan (or ramekins) on a wire rack for at least 30 minutes before serving.

Persian Rice

By Roya Hakakian

For all the love lavished upon lumpy Ashkenazi darlings such as the bagel, kugel, and matzo ball, it is indeed Persian rice that, if it came down to it, could serve as the Jewish people's most fitting alimentary metaphor. Lean, distinct grains, negligible on their own, become gastronomically substantial when together on a spoon or in a mound on the tray. Come what may, be it herb (dill, leek, parsley) or spice (cumin, cinnamon, cardamom) or bean (fava, green, or black-eyed pea) or fruit (raisin, barberry, cranberry), Persian rice blends them all into a sumptuous sum far greater than its separate parts.

While the palatable repast might lead the epicure to believe mere lightness accounts for the taste, the crusty, bottom-of-the-pot concoction offers a tough rebuttal, leaving room for many interpretations, for instance, this: Only with so hardened a bottom does such lightness on top become possible. And can one make this dish from a mere recipe? Queen Esther would advise against it, if she could. It takes serious dedication to learning by the side of a culinary chacham to create the crusty-fluffy paradox without involving the local fire chief, not so metaphorically speaking!

PERSIAN RICE

Serves 8 to 10

2½ cups (500 grams) white basmati rice, such as Lal Qilla

½ cup plus 1 tablespoon (69 grams) kosher salt

½ teaspoon saffron, crushed

1 large egg, lightly beaten

4 tablespoons plus 1½ teaspoons (67 milliliters) vegetable oil, such as canola or sunflower, plus more for drizzling

Place the rice in a large bowl and rinse with cold water four to five times, until the water runs clear. Drain the rice and transfer to a large bowl. Add 8 cups (2 liters) warm water and 6 tablespoons (46 grams) of the salt. Soak for at least 3 hours, or up to overnight. Drain the rice.

To cook the rice, use a three-to-one ratio of water to soaked rice. For 5 cups of soaked rice, bring 15 cups (3 liters plus 750 milliliters) water to a boil in a large pot. Add the remaining 3 tablespoons salt (23 grams), 1½ teaspoons (7 milliliters) oil, and the soaked rice. Return to a boil, then reduce the heat to medium-high, so the water is still boiling vigorously. Cook for 7 to 9 minutes, checking the rice after 5 minutes—when it's ready, it will be softened but still have some bite. Immediately drain the rice in a large colander and rinse with cold water.

Place the saffron in a bowl and steep in 1 tablespoon (15 milliliters) hot water. Add 1 cup of the drained rice, the egg, and ½ teaspoon of the oil. Stir to combine.

To get the crispy tahdig layer, in a tall, heavy-bottomed pot with a 9-inch base, add the remaining 3 tablespoons (45 milliliters) oil and heat over high heat until shimmering, about 2 minutes. Add the saffron mixture and spread evenly over the bottom of the pot. Lower the heat to medium-low and let the mixture crisp up, about 10 minutes.

Place the remaining rice over the tahdig in a mound, and drizzle some oil on top. Cook, uncovered, until steam is rising from the rice, 15 to 20 minutes, making sure that the tahdig does not burn. If you do not see steam rising from the rice, add a few tablespoons of hot water, and watch for the steam to develop.

Reduce the heat to the lowest setting, cover the top of the pot with a paper towel or clean kitchen towel, and close the lid for a tight seal. Cook until the rice is soft and fluffy, about 1 hour.

To serve, scoop all of the rice onto a platter. When you get to the golden layer, lift it from the bottom of the pot, break it up into pieces, and place on top of the rice.

Pickles

By Gail Simmons

As far back as I can remember, full-sour dill pickles have been the single most important food in my life. There's no other flavor as satisfying, or that defines my family and my Jewish heritage as perfectly, as a pickle. Allow me to explain: My mother was a fabulous cook. Growing up in Toronto, I was spoiled by the freshly made meals she prepared each day. My father, on the other hand, could barely boil water. But somehow he managed to become our family pickle maker. Each year in late summer, when Kirby cucumbers came into season, my father would drag home a giant bushel from the market, and for two days my mother's kitchen would become his pickling lab. I cannot imagine our fridge or cellar without a jar or twelve of his full-sour, dill-weed-infused, lip-smacking, face-puckering pickles. We ate them all year round, after school or as midnight snacks, with burgers or roast turkey, piled onto platters and served every Friday night for Shabbat, but also on Rosh Hashanah, Passover, and Hanukkah. No holiday table was complete without them.

In my early twenties, I moved to New York for culinary school. One afternoon, tired and homesick, I went to the Lower East Side looking for a pickle to curb my craving. After tasting a few from the area's last remaining pickle sellers, I landed on one that did the trick. It wasn't quite as sour as my father's; its crunchy exterior didn't give way to a softer, intensely fermented center exactly as I had hoped, but it came close. And so for the next ten years, I loyally schlepped jars home to my Chelsea apartment whenever time allowed. When I got married in 2008 (to a fellow pickle enthusiast), it seemed only fitting that my father make a hundred jars of pickles to give to our guests as a memento, but the logistics of importing so many pickles across the border in their precious liquid proved insurmountable. So I pleaded with my pickle dealer to sell me jars of his pickles to custom-label for the occasion. He reluctantly agreed, and the wedding went off without a hitch.

A few years later, my husband and I had a daughter. As I watched my friends struggle with picky eaters and infinite demands for candy and sweets, a slow and steady fear took hold. What if my child didn't like pickles? Thankfully, my husband's and my predisposed taste buds were passed down to yet another generation, and at five years old, my daughter counts pickles among her favorite foods. We eat them together when I get home from work, on every Jewish holiday, and whenever we see them on restaurant menus. She demands them in her lunch and once in a while for breakfast, too. I couldn't be more proud. She equates them with her grandfather, and I hope that in time, she will come to think of them as I do: as a vital link to our past and to the generations of Jewish pickle eaters who came before us.

$\longrightarrow$

HALF-SOUR PICKLES

Makes about 8 pickles

8 Kirby cucumbers (1 pound/455 grams),
  thoroughly rinsed

2 tablespoons plus 1 teaspoon (35 grams)
  kosher salt

1 quart (1 liter) filtered water

5 garlic cloves

3 or 4 sprigs dill

¼ teaspoon dill seed

¼ teaspoon celery seed

¼ teaspoon mustard seed

¼ teaspoon fennel seed

Soak the cucumbers in cold water for 30 minutes and make sure they are free of any grime or dirt. If you like, cut off the non-stem ends, as they often contain a chemical that can make the pickles mushy.

Make a brine by combining the salt and the filtered water in a large bowl. Stir until completely dissolved.

Pack the cucumbers and garlic into a clean 3-quart (3-liter) jar and pour the brine over, making sure the brine covers the cucumbers completely. Make extra brine and add to cover if there isn't enough. Add the dill sprigs, followed by the dill seed, celery seed, mustard seed, and fennel seed. Cover and refrigerate for 10 days before eating.

The pickles will keep in the refrigerator for up to 1 month.

FULL-SOUR PICKLES

Makes about 8 pickles

8 Kirby cucumbers (1 pound/455 grams), thoroughly rinsed

¼ cup (60 grams) kosher salt

1 quart (1 liter) filtered water

2 garlic cloves, smashed

4 sprigs dill

½ teaspoon dill seed (optional)

¼ teaspoon coriander seed (optional)

Soak the cucumbers in cold water for 30 minutes and make sure they are free of any grime or dirt. If you like, cut off the non-stem ends, as they often contain a chemical that can make the pickles mushy.

Make a brine by combining the salt and the filtered water in a large bowl. Stir until completely dissolved.

Pack the cucumbers and garlic into a clean 3-quart (3-liter) jar and pour the brine over, making sure the brine covers the cucumbers completely. Make extra brine and add to cover if there isn't enough. Add the dill sprigs and the dill and coriander seeds (if using) and, using a clean wooden spoon, swoosh them around to distribute.

Loosely cover the jar with a lid. Place a plate under the jar to catch any spillover and let the pickles stand at room temperature for 4 days. Every day, loosen the lid to "burp" the jar, then replace the lid to continue the fermentation. After 4 days, scoop out a pickle with a clean utensil, not with your fingers, and cut a piece to taste if it's sour enough for you—if it is, refrigerate immediately. If not, let the jar stand for up to 3 days more, tasting the pickles each day to see what tastes best to you. You should see the brine becoming cloudy and a few "lazy" bubbles forming here and there—this means you're on the right track. When the pickles are sour to your liking, seal the jar and store in the refrigerator. The pickles will keep in the fridge for up to 2 months.

Pkaila

By Liel Leibovitz

Think of *pkaila* as the hipster Jewish dream food: It's the greatest authentic dish you've never heard of. Enjoyed by Tunisian Jews—their Muslim neighbors still know nothing of the dish and its pleasures—it involves gargantuan amounts of spinach fried diligently until nearly charred and then stewed slowly with forgiving cuts of beef or lamb and a small white mountain of beans. Add a forest of cilantro and mint shortly before serving, and you have an aromatic mixture that is the perfect topping for a mound of couscous.

With so much of our contemporary culinary scene dedicated to the breaking down of cultural boundaries and the creation of new food fusions, it's delightful to see an unreconstructed dish, still unknown and untouched, belonging only to those who took the time and toiled to cook it on Rosh Hashanah and the occasional Shabbat. It's the opposite of that famous Levy's rye bread ad—you *do* have to be Jewish to love pkaila.

PKAILA

Serves 4 to 6

¼ cup (60 milliliters) olive oil

1 medium yellow onion, chopped

1 pound (455 grams) spinach, coarsely chopped

1½ teaspoons salt

2 teaspoons coarsely chopped fresh thyme

½ cup (15 grams) coarsely chopped fresh mint

1½ cups (75 grams) coarsely chopped fresh cilantro

¼ teaspoon ground cinnamon

1 tablespoon (2 grams) ground cumin

1 tablespoon (2 grams) ground coriander

2 garlic cloves, chopped

1 small red chile, such as Fresno, serrano, or similar, cut lengthwise

1 cup (262 grams) dried white beans, such as navy, cannellini, or similar, soaked overnight

6 to 7 cups (1.4 to 1.7 liters) chicken stock or water

2 pounds (900 grams) lamb shoulder or lamb stew, cut into 2-inch (5-centimeter) pieces

4 medium Yukon Gold potatoes (740 grams), peeled and halved

Preheat the oven to 300°F (148°C).

Heat the oil over medium high heat in a large heavy pot with a lid. Add the onion to the pot and cook until the onions are soft and fragrant but not changing color, about 5 minutes. Add the spinach, season with ½ teaspoon of the salt, and cook, stirring frequently, until wilted, about 3 minutes.

Add the thyme, mint, cilantro, cinnamon, cumin, coriander, garlic, chile, and white beans. Add the stock or water and the remaining 1 teaspoon salt and stir to combine. Add the meat and bring to a simmer.

Cover and move the pot to the oven. Cook covered for 30 minutes.

Add the potatoes to the pot, cover, and return to the oven for another hour. When the meat is fork tender and the beans and potatoes are cooked through, the dish is ready. Taste and adjust seasoning if needed and serve.

Pomegranates

By Dr. Ruth Westheimer

Pomegranate is one of the foods that are actually mentioned in the Bible. It has to do with *pru urvu*: the commandment to be fruitful and multiply. And it is a very sexy food—it's sweet and has little seeds in it, and it looks round, so I can understand why they thought it was a nice food for talking about multiplying. It also has 613 seeds, the number of bones in the human body. Some people also say pomegranates are good for fertility. I don't know if that's true or not. I do know that pomegranates are great, but it takes effort to eat one. That's definitely like good sex: It takes work for both to be good lovers.

A SCHMUTZ-FREE METHOD FOR SEEDING POMEGRANATES

Freeing the seeds from a pomegranate doesn't have to be a messy affair. It can actually be easy. Start by choosing a nice piece of fruit, one that's heavy for its size and has a deep-red hue. Place the pomegranate frilly-side up on a cutting board and, using a sharp knife, score the skin around the equator, taking care not to cut into the juicy seeds. Now pull the two halves apart with your hands. They should come apart without spilling any juice. Hold one pomegranate half, cut-side down, over a large bowl, and start tapping on the skin using the back of a metal or wooden spoon. The seeds will start dropping into the bowl. Tap all over until all the seeds are out, and repeat with the second half.

Poppy Seeds

By Gabriella Gershenson

Poppy seeds are hard-to-explain delicious—floral but gritty, welcome and yet peskily ever-present (especially between your teeth). Their taste is earthy, elemental. Sweet filling made from poppy seeds looks like potting soil; indeed, the actual seeds enter this world in the bellies of flowers. The crunchy, nutty specks are as much a source of texture and color as they are of flavor and, even more so, of identity.

Poppy seeds are a motif in the great foods of the Jewish canon, in hamantaschen (page 125), *flódni* (page 113), and yeast-dough strudels, on challahs (page 61), bialys (page 34), and bagels (page 29); and are eaten in places where Jews once thrived, from Alsace, France, to deep Russia. Though these communities are diminished or gone, that sprinkling of black seeds on your lap, in the bag your everything bagel came in, in the trendy halvah you smuggled home from Israel, are lingering reminders of who we are, a trail of where we came from.

MOHN KICHLACH (POPPY SEED COOKIES)
by Stacey Harwood-Lehman

Makes thirty-six 1½-inch or forty-eight 1-inch cookies

2 large eggs, at room temperature

½ cup (100 grams) sugar

⅓ cup (80 milliliters) vegetable oil

2½ cups (315 grams) unbleached all-purpose flour, plus more for rolling

¼ cup (40 grams) poppy seeds

¾ teaspoon baking powder

Pinch of kosher salt

1 large egg yolk

1 tablespoon (30 milliliters) water

In the bowl of a stand mixer fitted with the whisk attachment, beat the eggs and sugar on medium speed for about 3 minutes, until pale yellow. Continue beating while adding the oil in a thin, steady stream, beating until the oil is incorporated.

Combine the flour, poppy seeds, baking powder, and salt in a medium bowl, and using a whisk, mix until the ingredients are evenly distributed throughout.

Stop the mixer, then add the dry ingredients to the egg mixture. Turn the mixer speed to low and mix until the dough just comes together. The dough should have the consistency of rich tart dough—pliable and moist, not dry or sticky.

Turn the dough out onto a piece of plastic wrap, shape it into a ball, flatten it slightly to get a thick disk, and refrigerate for 1 hour or up to 24 hours.

When ready to bake, position a rack in the center of the oven and preheat the oven to 350°F (177°C). Line a cookie sheet with parchment paper.

Whisk the egg yolk with the water in a small bowl.

Roll the dough out into a 9 by 13-inch (23 by 33-centimeter) rectangle on a floured board with a floured rolling pin. Trim the ragged edges of the rectangle using a paring knife or a pizza cutter, then cut the dough into 1-inch squares, or 1½ inches for a slightly larger cookie. Generously brush the squares with the egg wash and, using a small offset spatula, transfer to the cookie sheet. Bake for about 16 minutes, or until slightly puffed and golden around the edges. The cookies should be glistening from the egg wash. Transfer the cookies to a wire rack and let cool completely. The cookies will harden as they cool.

Potatoes

By Elissa Goldstein

If there's a case to be made for a single ingredient as one of the greatest Jewish foods of all time, allow me to make it for the potato. Adaptable, humble, and comforting, it's an essential ingredient in many classic Jewish dishes: Sabbath stews, latkes, kugel, *burekas*, even fish and chips.

The potato transcends geography, class, and language. Ask a Jew about potatoes (really, it's a great icebreaker) and they will tell you a story—about the scraps that sustained their ancestors through a war or a perilous journey, about the creamy chunks in their savta's *hamin*, about the pleasure of a perfectly boiled Yukon Gold dipped in salt water at the beginning of the Seder meal. Someone will sing "Bulbes," the classic Yiddish folk song about the quotidian tediousness of a potato-based diet. The potato is the Jewish ingredient ne plus ultra—it evokes notions of family, ritual, suffering, and history. Case closed.

LATKES
by Alison Cayne

Makes sixteen to twenty 4-inch (10-centimeter) pancakes

3 Idaho russet potatoes, peeled

1 large egg, whisked

Fine sea salt

Extra-virgin olive oil, for frying

Flaky sea salt, such as Maldon, to finish

OPTIONAL BONUSES

¼ cup (32 grams) sliced or diced onion

¼ cup (14 grams) chopped fresh chives

Set up a landing station next to your frying area: Place a wire rack on a baking sheet and have a spatula handy.

Using the large holes of a box grater, grate the potatoes into a large bowl. (Alternatively, grate the potatoes using a food processor fitted with the shredding blade.) You should have about 4 cups shredded potatoes. Wrap the potatoes in a kitchen towel and squeeze out the excess moisture; squeezing should generate about ½ cup (120 milliliters) of liquid. The potatoes may turn a bit reddish-brown.

Put the potatoes back in the bowl. Add the egg and a large pinch of salt (the optional onion or chives can be added at this point) and mix the ingredients to combine.

Heat ¼ to ½ inch (6 millimeters to 1.5 centimeters) of oil in a large sauté pan over medium-high heat. When the oil begins to shimmer, start forming the patties. (You can test the temperature by putting the handle of a wooden spoon or a wooden chopstick into the oil; if the oil is hot, bubbles will form around it.)

Using your nondominant hand, scoop up about ⅓ cup (75 grams) of the potato mixture. Use the side of the bowl to help form the mixture into a patty. Drain any excess liquid into the bowl and gently lay the patty in the hot oil. Keep your other hand clean and dry so you can use your spatula and grab a towel if needed. Gently press the latke with the spatula until evenly flat. Repeat to make a few more patties, taking care not to crowd the pan. Fry until the edges brown and get lacy, 2 to 3 minutes. Flip and cook for 2 to 3 minutes more, until browned on the second side. Continually monitor and adjust the temperature of the oil while frying; too-hot oil will result in burnt edges and raw middles. Use the spatula to transfer the latkes to the wire rack, sprinkle with flaky sea salt, and serve hot.

Before frying the next batch, check your oil: If it is dark brown, smells, or is filled with burnt bits, ditch it and start with fresh oil. Wipe down the pan with paper towels, taking care not to burn yourself, then add more oil to coat the bottom again, heat the oil, and fry the remaining patties.

Ptcha

By Michael Twitty

As an African American Jewish culinary historian, I would like to think I know something about soul food. Just as *gribenes* (page 120) are analogous to cracklings, the Jewish soul food equivalent of chitlins—the small intestine of the pig consumed during slaughtering time by enslaved people on Southern plantations—is a little gem known as *ptcha*. Never heard of it? Well, your family's relationship with Jell-O, jelly rings, and the like started with this Eastern European Jewish delicacy, the jellied feet of calves. Despite the fact that most commercial gelatin isn't kosher, Jews had their own jelly fascinations.

Ptcha, a word derived from Turkish, is just one of several regional terms, including *fisnoga*, *sulz*, and *holodets*, for this formerly popular Sabbath delicacy. The feet were boiled and served in their own aspic and flavored with as much garlic and onion as possible. Ptcha can in fact be seen as a means to ingest an enormous amount of garlic without being viewed as ostensibly meshuga, just as gefilte fish is just a vehicle for shoveling in as much horseradish as humanly possible.

Ptcha was popular because the feet symbolized, for peasants, the truth of Torah and Yiddishkeit, especially during the rise of Hasidism. *Sheker*, or "a lie" in Hebrew, teeters on one leg, while *emes*, or "truth," solidly stands on four feet . . . kind of like a cow.

One can imagine how popular ptcha would have been. It used up a part of the animal perhaps considered inedible. The natural gelatin and fat kept it safe overnight in the days before refrigeration. The onion and garlic not only added antiseptic powers, unbeknownst to the shtetl, but also provided essential nutrients that staved off deficiencies like scurvy. Ptcha was what much soul food is about: rescued odds and ends turned into a delicacy with symbolic meanings that turn out to have real benefits. If, that is, you can eat past the no-thank-you bite.

Rye Bread

By Ruth Reichl

My father arrived in America in 1926. He was twenty-six years old, and he carried three things with him: a doctorate in German literature, a burning desire to work in publishing, and an utter contempt for American food.

He never changed. Dad looked at the cereal Mom and I occasionally breakfasted upon with loathing. He considered salad strange. The only vegetable that ever crossed his plate was red cabbage (preferably with sauerbraten). And although he was a gentle man, he refused to partake of any meal that lacked a basket of bread.

"Not those fluffy white slices that evaporate in your mouth," Dad said contemptuously. He wanted sturdy stuff you could sink your teeth into, a loaf with heft, color, and character. To please him, Mom went to the bakery every morning for a fresh loaf of seeded corn rye. There is no corn in corn rye; *Korn* is the medieval German term for "grain," but in bread it almost always refers to rye. The seeded corn ryes of my childhood were sourdough loaves, yeasty, light, and so rich with caraway seeds that their fragrance perfumed the entire table.

I hated that bread. It was embarrassing to show up at school with a lunchbox filled with thick sandwiches on mismatched slices that permeated the lunchroom with their telltale scent. I longed for the pristine square sandwiches other moms made, those clean, white envelopes with their innocent airs. I swore that when I grew up, I would never eat another slice of rye. But as New York's German population faded away and its Jews assimilated, their breads began to vanish. Corn rye became a thing of the past, and to my surprise, I missed it.

Happily, the artisan-bread movement has started bringing the old loaves back, and I find myself buying corn rye with increasing frequency, so eager for that familiar flavor that the loaf's half gone before I reach home. It is, I realize, the taste of my childhood. And it occurs to me that, in this case, Father really did know best.

Sabich

By Liel Leibovitz

Israelis, too impatient for leisurely lunches, stuff their midday meals in a pita. Sometimes it's falafel, sometimes it's shawarma, and on particularly decadent days, it's a nobly proportioned and golden schnitzel. But no dish rivets the attention and excites more than *sabich*, a fried eggplant with a hard-boiled egg, tahini, pickles, and a pungent mango chutney known as *amba*.

Like everything else in Israel that merits true religious devotion, the origins of sabich are controversial. Some say the dish was a popular breakfast back in Iraq, and that the name is a variation on the Arabic word for "morning," *sabach*. Others believe the dish got its name from its originator, an Iraqi Jewish immigrant named Sabich who opened up a small shop in Ramat Gan in 1961 to sell his magical creation.

Either way, the sabich proved to be a stroke of daring genius, a taste, quite literally, of Start-up Nation avant la lettre—cheap to make, quick to assemble, and packed with flavor. So absolute is the dish's dominance on the local food scene that it taught Israelis, notoriously allergic to orderly lines, how to queue up.

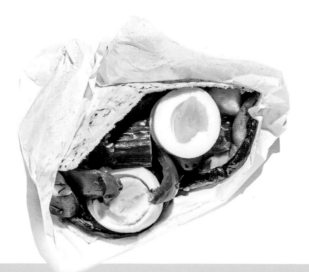

HOW TO ORDER AT OVED'S, ISRAEL'S GREATEST SABICH JOINT

Givatayim, a sleepy suburb of Tel Aviv, isn't the sort of place you'd think would be home to a true culinary temple, but drive down its main thoroughfare on any given afternoon and you'll see cars triple-parked and people lined up quietly, a rarity for Israelis, waiting for the eponymous Oved to work his magic. Other joints can cook up a decent sabich, but only Oved can put on a show, turning the assembly of fried eggplant, tahini, and a hard-boiled egg in a pita into something halfway between a Broadway show and a pagan ritual. When it's finally your turn, Oved will eye you and ask one crucial question: What's the score in the Derby? The Derby is the annual match between Tel Aviv's two rival soccer teams: Hapoel, which wears red uniforms, and Maccabi, decked out in yellow. What Oved is really asking is for you to tell him how much *schug* and how much *amba* you'd like in your pita: *schug*, a Yemenite hot pepper spread, is red, and *amba*, an Indian mango chutney, is yellow. Tell Oved that the Derby was tied one to one, and you'll get a spoonful of each. Say Maccabi beat Hapoel three to nothing, and you'll get a pungent but not too spicy sandwich. Stare Oved in the eye uncomprehendingly, and fifty irate and hungry Israelis standing behind you on line will tell you exactly what they think about your inability to make a decision.

Liel Leibovitz

→

SABICH
by Einat Admony

Serves 4 to 6

2 large eggplant, stem ends trimmed

Kosher salt

Canola oil, for frying

1 cup (145 grams) finely chopped unpeeled
   cucumber

1 cup (240 grams) finely chopped tomato

3 tablespoons (12 grams) finely chopped
   fresh parsley

3 tablespoons (18 grams) chopped
   scallions (optional)

Freshly ground black pepper

4 to 6 pita loaves

Hummus (page 143)

Huevos Haminados (page 131) or hard-
   boiled eggs, thinly sliced

Amba Sauce (recipe follows)

Tahini Sauce (recipe follows)

Peel strips of skin lengthwise off the eggplant ¼ inch (6 millimeters) apart. Slice the eggplant into ¼-inch-thick (6-millimeter) rounds and generously salt each piece. Place the eggplant in a colander in the sink to drain for about 1 hour.

Heat ¼ inch (6 millimeters) of canola oil in a deep skillet until it reaches about 375°F (190°C). Pat the eggplant dry with a few sheets of paper towels. Working in small batches, fry the eggplant in the hot oil until golden brown. Transfer the fried eggplant to paper towels to drain and set aside.

Toss together the cucumber, tomato, parsley, and scallions (if using) in a large bowl until well combined. Season the Israeli salad with a little salt and pepper and set aside.

To assemble the sabich, cut an opening at one end of a pita bread to make a pocket. Smear the inside of the pita pocket with hummus, then place a spoonful of the Israeli salad at the bottom. Add one slice of fried eggplant, a few slices of the egg, and then another spoonful of the Israeli salad. Top it off with another piece of eggplant, a few more slices of egg, a spoonful of amba sauce, and some tahini sauce. Repeat with the remaining pita breads.

If you have any eggplant left over, slather some tahini on it. You can never have too much eggplant.

Amba Sauce

Makes about 5 cups (1.2 liters)

6 large yellow mangoes

¼ cup plus 2 tablespoons (90 grams) kosher salt

⅓ cup plus 3 tablespoons (110 milliliters) canola oil

1 medium yellow onion, finely chopped

¾ cup (132 grams) mustard seeds

¼ cup (32 grams) cumin seeds

2 tablespoons (14 grams) sweet Hungarian paprika

1 tablespoon (6 grams) ground fenugreek

1 tablespoon plus 1 teaspoon (8 grams) ground turmeric

1 tablespoon (5 grams) coriander seeds

12 garlic cloves, finely chopped

½ cup (120 milliliters) white wine vinegar

Peel the mangoes and cut them into strips about the size of your pinky. Salt them thoroughly and place them in a large canning jar or glass baking dish. Cover tightly and allow to ferment for 5 days, preferably in the hot sun.

After 5 days, drain the mangoes in a colander set over a bowl; reserve the juices. Scatter the mangoes over a baking sheet and allow them to dry for 4 to 5 hours.

Heat 3 tablespoons (45 milliliters) of canola oil in a large pot over medium heat. Add the onion and cook, stirring, until golden brown, about 7 minutes. Add the mustard seeds, cumin seeds, paprika, fenugreek, turmeric, coriander seeds, and garlic. Cook, stirring, for 2 minutes, then add the reserved mango juices. Bring to a simmer, then remove from the heat. Stir in the vinegar and mangoes until well combined. Let the mixture cool to room temperature.

Transfer the cooled mango mixture to a food processor and pulse just until the mangoes are finely chopped. You're looking for a chunky sauce rather than a puree. Transfer the amba sauce to a jar with a tight-fitting lid and top off with the remaining ⅓ cup (120 milliliters) oil.

This sauce will keep in the refrigerator for at least 6 months.

Tahini Sauce

Makes about 1½ cups (360 milliliters)

½ cup (120 milliliters) tahini

½ cup (120 milliliters) water, plus more as needed

⅓ cup (80 milliliters) fresh lemon juice

1 garlic clove

2 teaspoons kosher salt

Combine the tahini, water, lemon juice, garlic, and salt in a food processor. Process until smooth and creamy.

Schmaltz

By Jeffrey Yoskowitz

Schmaltz, or rendered poultry fat, was once considered so valuable to Jews in Eastern and Central Europe as a critical cooking fat that they stored it in vessels secured with padlocks. For most of the '80s, '90s, and aughts, however, you couldn't give the stuff away.

Central and Eastern European Jews once cooked nearly exclusively with butter and schmaltz: the yin and yang of the kosher kitchen. For fleishig meals (which include meat), especially in late fall, winter, and spring, schmaltz was the go-to. The advent of vegetable and canola oils and new products like Crisco vegetable shortening didn't help. The twentieth century may be known for an intellectual flourishing of the American Jewish community, but it should also be known as the century that rendered flavorful Jewish dishes and desserts a distant memory.

I didn't cook with schmaltz until I was in my twenties. As soon as I began rendering my own from chicken or goose fat, cooking with schmaltz added new layers of flavor and new depths to the Ashkenazi dishes I began to prepare. I felt like my parents and teachers had lied to me about the dreariness of Jewish food. "Jewish cooking today has a reputation for blandness, not entirely unearned," Jane Ziegelman writes in *97 Orchard*, her impressive culinary history of the tenements on the Lower East Side. "A hundred years ago, however, the label would have never stuck." The disappearance of schmaltz isn't the only reason for the poor reputation of Jewish food these days, but it's a pretty obvious one.

Thankfully, due to the erosion of accepted midcentury nutritional dogma, saturated fats are considered "in." And, just like that, schmaltz—and the distinctly Jewish flavors it bestows—is again on the menu.

$\longrightarrow$

SCHMALTZ

Makes ⅔ cup (160 milliliters)

1 pound (455 grams) chicken fat and skin, collected from 3 to 4 pounds (1.4 to 1.8 kilograms) chicken thighs

1 teaspoon kosher salt

3 tablespoons (45 milliliters) cold water

1 large onion, halved lengthwise and thinly sliced (about 2 cups)

Wash the chicken fat and skin in cold water, drain well, and blot dry with a paper towel. Cut the fat and skin into ½-inch (1.5-centimeter) pieces. To make it easier to cut, freeze the chicken fat and skin for at least 2 hours before cutting.

Place the chicken fat and skin in a large skillet and season with ½ teaspoon of the salt. Add the water and bring to a simmer over medium heat. Reduce the heat to low and cook, stirring occasionally and scraping the bottom of the pan to loosen any browned bits, until the water has evaporated, the fat starts to render, and the pieces of fat and skin start to brown, curl up, and shrink to about half their size, about 30 minutes.

Add the sliced onion and the remaining ½ teaspoon salt and cook until the onion softens and caramelizes, about 35 minutes. Lower the heat if needed to prevent the onion or chicken skin from overbrowning, which will affect the color of the schmaltz (it should be golden).

Strain the schmaltz through a fine-mesh strainer set over a large bowl; set the solids aside (see Note). Use the schmaltz immediately, or let cool to room temperature, then transfer to a jar with a lid and refrigerate. The schmaltz will keep in the refrigerator for 3 to 4 days or in the freezer for up to 2 months.

NOTE: The solids in the strainer are the gribenes (page 120). Eat them as a snack, add them to chopped liver (page 86), or sprinkle them over salad. They will keep in an airtight container in the refrigerator for 3 to 4 days or in the freezer for up to 2 months.

Seltzer

By Wayne Hoffman

Only two kinds of people truly love seltzer: Jews and clowns.

Clowns spray it to get a laugh; Jews don't need to—we have good timing. But for Jews, seltzer is not to be wasted. "Seltzer is for drinking, not for spraying," as Rabbi Hyman Krustofsky, voiced by Jackie Mason, explained to his son, Herschel, on *The Simpsons*. More diet than diet cola, more bubbly than "bubbly," it's the thing that turns delicious but goyish chocolate milk into a proper egg cream.

The "2-cents plain" costs a lot more than it used to, though, and that's a problem for people who go through a lot of seltzer. (Herschel Krustofsky, for instance, grew up to become Krusty, a Jew *and* a clown; he rigged up a spritzer to his doorbell, so you can imagine his seltzer bills.) The solution comes from what was the hottest kitchen appliance of the twenty-first century until the Instant Pot came along: the SodaStream, which turns every kitchen into a soda fountain. Made in Israel, of course. No joke.

Shakshuka

By Liel Leibovitz

So what if the Moroccans make it, too. Never mind that the Tunisians eat it for breakfast each weekend, or that it delights the Greeks and satiates the Algerians: *Shakshuka* is Israeli now. In fact, it's Israeli because, not in spite, of its widespread popularity across the Middle East.

As Jews huddled for safety in their biblical homeland, fleeing violence in Rabat or Tunis or Algiers, they could take comfort in one thing: simmering onions, peppers, and tomatoes, topped with a couple of eggs, cooked in a skillet and consumed with a fresh loaf of white bread. It was what home tasted like, no matter where home happened to be.

The ingredients are so basic and the flavors so recognizable that these days, if you want to evoke the mists of the Mediterranean in Boston or Berlin, all you have to do is whip up a skillet of shakshuka. For a true melting-pot experience, some add griddled Cypriot halloumi cheese.

⟶

SHAKSHUKA
by Einat Admony

Serves 4 to 6

3 tablespoons (45 milliliters) canola oil

2 medium yellow onions, chopped

1 large green bell pepper, cored, seeded, and chopped

1 large jalapeño, cored, seeded, and chopped

7 garlic cloves, finely chopped

¼ cup (60 milliliters) tomato paste

1 (28-ounce/793-gram) can whole peeled tomatoes, crushed by hand

1 bay leaf

2½ tablespoons (32 grams) sugar

1½ tablespoons (23 grams) kosher salt

1 tablespoon (7 grams) sweet Hungarian paprika

1 tablespoon (6 grams) ground cumin

1½ teaspoons freshly ground black pepper

1 teaspoon ground caraway seeds

½ bunch Swiss chard, stemmed, leaves chopped, or spinach

8 to 12 large eggs

Heat the canola oil in a large skillet over medium heat. Add the onions and cook until translucent, 5 to 10 minutes. Add the bell pepper and jalapeño and cook until just softened, 3 to 5 minutes. Stir in the garlic and tomato paste and cook, stirring, for 2 minutes more.

Slowly pour in the tomatoes. Stir in the bay leaf, sugar, salt, paprika, cumin, black pepper, and caraway and simmer for 20 minutes. Layer the Swiss chard leaves on top.

Crack the eggs into the tomato mixture. Cover and simmer for about 10 minutes, or until the whites of the eggs are no longer translucent.

Slivovitz

By Michael Wex

When I was growing up among Polish Jews in western Canada, the main shul shot was rye. Crown Royal on special occasions. Once in a while, scotch. So what made slivovitz, a plum brandy rough enough to make Frankie Valli *krekhts* (groan) like Tom Waits, so Jewish, even to those of us who rarely drank it? It embodied a worldview. As my grandfather once put it, "You don't have to like it. You just have to remember that it's the one thing you buy in a store that doesn't taste worse on Pesach." It didn't have to be good; it only had to be not worse.

What can you say but amen?

Sofrito

By Rachel Figueroa de Zimmerman

Every Friday, the aroma of simmering onions, cumin, turmeric, peppers, and garlic wafts up from Jewish stovetops throughout the world. For the people in these homes, *sofrito*—a dish with roots dating back to the Roman Empire—serves as a reminder of the impending Sabbath.

For non-Jews in Puerto Rico and other parts of Latin America, sofrito refers to only the sauce, or a base used for cooking. For Sephardim, sofrito is the final product—the full dish. As a Puerto Rican Jew, I keep a Tupperware full of sofrito in my freezer that I use to make . . . sofrito.

Sofrito can be made with almost anything. The word *sofrito* comes from the Spanish *sofreír*, which means "to fry lightly." As such, most sofrito recipes involve sautéing a protein, peppers, potatoes, and herbs and spices in olive oil. Some recipes even call for deep-frying some of the ingredients before incorporating them into the stew. In a lot of ways, sofrito is like cholent. It's something you can cook and keep heated on Friday and eat throughout Shabbat. With sofrito, however, the cooking time is much shorter. If you're feeling spicy, you can throw some cumin, coriander, and other spices into your cholent and have yourself a sofrito-fusion Sephardic Sabbath.

But how did this humble dish of Spanish origin grow to become one of the universal culinary truths—one that ties together kitchens all throughout the Sephardic Diaspora?

$\longrightarrow$

Well, in 1492 Columbus sailed over here with a bunch of Jews—refugees from the quarter-million-strong community that had just been expelled from Spain. In 1536, the Portuguese followed suit with an inquisition of their own. With that, the Sephardic community, its culture, and its cuisine spread across the globe. Sofrito went from Iberian to international.

The traditional recipe for sofrito? It depends on whom you ask. One person might tell you that the base for a traditional sofrito contains tomatoes. A second might tell you that since tomatoes are a New World fruit, they don't belong in there at all. The first will then retort that the New World was colonized over five hundred years ago, and that's long enough for something to become a tradition.

As the old saying goes, "Two Jews, three sofritos."

SOFRITO

3 tablespoons (45 milliliters) olive oil

1 (4-pound/1.8-kilogram) chicken, quartered, plus wings

Kosher salt and freshly ground black pepper

1 large onion, halved and thickly sliced

5 or 6 garlic cloves

4 medium carrots, cut into 1½-inch (4-centimeter) pieces

1 large celery stalk, finely diced

Juice of 1 lemon

1 teaspoon ground turmeric

4 cardamom pods, cracked

1 cup (240 milliliters) water

Cooked rice, for serving

Heat the oil in a large pan over medium-high heat until almost smoking.

Meanwhile, pat the chicken dry with paper towels and season it generously with salt and pepper. Carefully (to avoid the spattering oil) place the chicken flat in the pan, skin-side down, and sear until golden brown, about 5 minutes. Transfer the chicken to a plate and set aside.

Add the onion and garlic to the pan and cook, stirring, until the onion starts to take on color, about 5 minutes. Add the carrots and celery and cook, stirring, until the celery begins to soften, about 2 minutes.

Return the chicken to the pan, skin-side up. Add the lemon juice, turmeric, cardamom, 2 teaspoons salt, ¾ teaspoon pepper, and water and bring to a boil. Reduce the heat to low, cover, and cook, turning the chicken over every 5 minutes or so and adding water as necessary, until the chicken is very tender, about 45 minutes. There should be a good amount of sauce.

Transfer the chicken to a plate, cover to keep the chicken moist, and simmer the sauce until it thickens, about 20 minutes more. Return the chicken to the pan, cover the pan, and simmer for 10 minutes to rewarm the chicken. Serve hot, accompanied by cooked rice.

Soup Mandel

By Gil Hovav

Let's face it: Israelis think they invented everything. Everything! Stents? It was us. Cherry tomatoes? Us again. Disk on key? Yup. Sliced bread? Sure. And don't forget rice (and God!).

But when it comes to *soup mandel*, we may have taken it a bit too far. While the Yiddishe name implies that this godly creation was made for chicken soup, which we invented (hey, we invented chickens!), the old *mameloshen* name also means that the roots of the mandel are in Europe and not Israel.

Well, this may be the case, but we Israelis have improved it. Our *shkedei marak* ("soup almonds" in Hebrew) are smaller, baked and not fried, and so shiny yellow that you may want to put on sunglasses before you eat them. Up until not too long ago, this was due to frightening contents of something that gave Israeli shkedei marak a lovely look of nuclear waste. Now it is all natural (but still more than 25 percent fat)—seven thousand tiny, crunchy squares of yellow happiness in every package.

Stella D'oro Swiss Fudge Cookies

By Ian Frazier

In 1930, 49 percent of the 1,265,258 people who lived in the Bronx were Jews. In certain parts, such as along Tremont Avenue, the figure was as high as 80 percent. A market for a certain kind of cookie was just sitting there—hundreds of thousands of cups of tea and coffee with nothing quite right to go with them. The Stella D'oro Bakery, a Bronx-based, family-owned company, saw the need and began to make Old World, less-sweet cookies from recipes that contained no dairy products. In America, the land of milk and cookies, Stella D'oro baked for the tea- and coffee-drinking, kosher-keeping connoisseur.

It succeeded gigantically. The Stella D'oro Swiss Fudge Cookie—about the size of a silver dollar, with a floral shape and a dark chocolate center that resembled the center of a sunflower—became the most Jewish cookie ever made.

By the 1950s, Stella D'oro had built a factory at the corner of 237th Street and Broadway, in the Kingsbridge section of the Bronx. The smell of baking cookies levitated the neighborhood for miles around. Depending on the wind and what was in production that day, you could smell the cinnamon, chocolate, and licorice (for the anisette toast) two el-train stops away.

The Zambetti family, which owned the company, prospered through two generations. In the 1980s, Stella D'oro was doing $65 million of business a year. Workers received top wages and put their kids through college. A Zambetti grandson, Marc, who was in his twenties, prepared to take the helm. Then, on October 17, 1989, Marc died in the San Francisco earthquake. The family sold the company, which soon became part of Kraft Foods. New management decided that not using dairy products was too expensive, so it changed the recipe and removed the pareve label. Rabbis wrote outraged letters. Sales fell by almost 50 percent. The old recipe was restored and the label put back on. Later, a hedge fund bought the company and cut salaries. The workers went on strike for eleven months but lost their jobs anyway when a North Carolina–based snack-food company bought Stella D'oro and moved it out of the Bronx. Stella D'oro's delicious baking smells now drift forlornly across the fields and through the woods of semirural Ashland, Ohio. The packages still say "pareve," and the cookies still taste the same. That the Swiss Fudge Cookie has its own story of suffering, exile, and survival makes it even more Jewish, I believe.

Stuffed Cabbage

By Michael Wex

Poles eat it, Czechs eat it, other Slavs and even Teutons eat it, but that doesn't alter the fact that stuffed cabbage taught me the difference between *treyf* (page 264) and goyish, the not-kosher and the not-Jewish. While trying to ease my way into eating pork, I ordered some cabbage rolls in a lard-in-everything-but-the-coffee Hungarian restaurant near the University of Toronto, but the sour cream atop those *haleptses* was so outrageous, so viscerally wrong as to drive me from my dreamt-of *treyf*. I bolted from the restaurant, more kosher than when I went in. *Khazer* was *khazer*, but for this, there were no words.

STUFFED CABBAGE

Makes about 16 rolls; serves 6

1 head green or savoy cabbage (about 4½ pounds/2 kilograms)

3 quarts (3 liters) boiling water

3 tablespoons (45 milliliters) olive oil

1 medium onion, chopped small

1½ teaspoons kosher salt, plus more as needed

3 medium carrots, parsnips, or a combination, shredded

1 celery stalk, finely chopped

Freshly ground black pepper

½ cup (110 grams) uncooked white rice

½ cup (75 grams) golden raisins

3 tablespoons (45 milliliters) tomato paste

1 pound (455 grams) ground beef

3 cups (720 milliliters) pureed tomatoes or tomato juice

Carve the core out of the cabbage using a sharp knife; leave the cabbage whole. Transfer the cabbage, cored-side up, to a large bowl and pour the boiling water over it. Cover and let the cabbage soften, about 15 minutes. Turn the cabbage over so the cored side is now on the bottom, cover, and let sit for 15 minutes more.

Heat the olive oil in a large skillet over medium heat. When the oil is shimmering, add the onion and cook, stirring, until softened, about 5 minutes. Season with a small pinch of salt. Add the carrots and/or parsnips and the celery and cook, stirring, until softened, about 5 minutes more. Season with another pinch of salt and some pepper, then transfer to a large bowl. Add the rice, raisins, and tomato paste to the bowl. Stir until the ingredients are mixed and let cool. Add the meat, season with 1½ teaspoons salt and more pepper, and mix to combine.

Drain the cabbage. Pull off the large leaves and cut out the large vein-like center rib. If the leaves are very large, you can halve them; if the leaves are smaller, remove the vein by partially cutting into the leaf. Pat the leaves dry with paper towels. Spoon about ¼ cup (60 grams) of the filling onto each leaf, on the part of the leaf that is the thinnest and most tender (the part farthest from the base of the leaf), then roll it up, tucking the sides in. Arrange the rolls, seam-side down, in a large, wide pot. If you need to layer the rolls, that's OK. Add the pureed tomatoes, then add 1 to 2 cups (240 to 480 milliliters) water to the puree container and swirl it around. Add enough liquid from the puree container to just cover the rolls (you may not need to add it all).

Set the pot over medium heat and bring to a lively simmer. Reduce the heat to low, cover, and simmer until the cabbage leaves become translucent and almost glass-like with shine, about 1 hour 15 minutes. Serve the rolls warm, with the sauce spooned over the top. Stuffed cabbage freezes beautifully—tightly cover the rolls and freeze for up to 3 months.

Sufganiyot

By Yotam Ottolenghi

A greasy, tacky, sugary oddball, injected with smooth, gummy red jam that hasn't seen a single berry in its life: This could easily be shortlisted for the worst Jewish foods, quite possibly topping the list (though for that, we have gefilte fish—page 114).

In reality, a *sufganiyah* can be as good or as bad as the quality of storytelling of the Hanukkah tale: a compelling plot of lights and splendor or a dubious account of a highly improbable episode. A good sufganiyah, when you come across it, is a magnificent miracle of billowy lightness accentuated by a creamy or fruity filling. Together, they form a truly irresistible package—against all odds!

WHY JEWS EAT FRIED FOODS ON HANUKKAH

Hanukkah, Hebrew for "dedication," is an eight-day-long celebration commemorating the rededication of the Second Temple in the second century BCE and the Maccabees' uprising against the Greeks. After defeating Antiochus and his Hellenizing forces, the Maccabees— Mattathias the Hasmonean and his five sons: Jochanan, Simeon, Eleazar, Jonathan, and Judah, who led the charge—recaptured the Temple, and set out to purge it of idols.

According to the Talmud, the Maccabees wished to light the Temple's menorah, a traditional candelabrum that customarily burned through the night in Judaism's holiest place, but discovered just enough oil to last for one day. Miraculously, however, the oil burned for eight days, a wonder we commemorate by lighting candles for eight nights. And, of course, by eating fried foods, like latkes and *sufganiyot*.

$\longrightarrow$

SUFGANIYOT
by Joan Nathan

Makes about 36 doughnuts

1 tablespoon (10 grams) active dry yeast

3 tablespoons (38 grams) granulated sugar

¼ cup (60 milliliters) water

½ cup (120 milliliters) lukewarm milk

1 large egg

1 large egg yolk

Pinch of kosher salt

Finely grated zest of 1 lemon

3½ cups (435 grams) unbleached all-purpose flour, plus more for dusting

3½ tablespoons (48 grams) unsalted butter, at room temperature

Vegetable oil, for deep-frying

1 cup (240 milliliters) raspberry, apricot, strawberry, or any flavorful jam, dulce de leche, Nutella, or lemon curd

Confectioners' or granulated sugar, for rolling and dusting

In a large bowl, dissolve the yeast and 1 tablespoon (12 grams) of the granulated sugar in the water, then stir in the milk.

Add the egg, egg yolk, salt, lemon zest, flour, remaining 2 tablespoons (26 grams) granulated sugar, and the butter. Mix with your hands until a dough forms, then knead the dough on a clean countertop until the dough is sticky and elastic.

Transfer the dough to a clean, lightly oiled bowl, cover with plastic wrap or a clean kitchen towel, and let rise in a warm place for at least 1 hour, until doubled in volume. If you want, you can let the dough rise overnight in the refrigerator; let it come to room temperature before rolling and cutting.

Dust a clean work surface with flour. Roll the dough out to a ½-inch (1.5-centimeter) thickness. Using the top of a glass or a biscuit cutter, cut out rounds about 2 inches (5 centimeters) wide and let rise for 30 minutes.

Heat at least 2 inches (5 centimeters) of vegetable oil in a heavy-bottomed pot over medium heat until it reaches 375°F (190°C) or is about to bubble.

Drop the doughnuts, 4 or 5 at a time, into the hot oil. Cook for 2 to 3 minutes on each side, turning when brown. You should see diminished bubbling and hear less sizzling when the doughnuts are ready to turn. Transfer to paper towels to drain. Repeat to fry the remaining doughnuts.

Using a pastry or cupcake injector (available at cooking stores and online), fill each doughnut with about 1 teaspoon of jam. Roll the sufganiyot in confectioners' or granulated sugar and serve immediately.

Sugar Cereals for Shabbos Morning

By Menachem Butler

The smell of freshly baked challah reminds me of my mother's challah, which she lovingly baked for each Shabbos when I was growing up. But it is another Shabbos delicacy from my childhood that taught me to honor the Sabbath with unique food. I refer to Rice Krispies, Honey Nut Cheerios, and other sugar cereals that my siblings and I (and, I assume, many others who grew up in the Orthodox Jewish community) were permitted to eat only on Saturday morning—as a replacement for the hot breakfasts that couldn't be cooked because of Sabbath prohibitions. While we woke up early to attend shul, it was unimaginable that we would leave the house until after we had eaten our special treat. As I got older and replaced eating sugar cereals before davening with the kiddush that followed, I remember with fondness my youthful excitement at awaking each Saturday morning to observe and remember the Sabbath by making it holy . . . with Froot Loops.

Sweet'N Low

By Daphne Merkin

These little pink packets with a musical staff logo containing powdered substitute sugar made largely from granulated saccharin are the perfect answer to fooling one's sweet tooth. Not for purists or the health-conscious, but for every woman who wanted to have her cake or coffee without sacrificing her waistline. First introduced in 1957 by a Jewish father-and-son team, over 500 billion packets have been produced to date. Think of them as a wink, a sly way of bypassing the confinement of the caloric laws with no loss in taste—an *eruv* guarding against fatty expansion.

Even today, the iconic pink packet stands its ground in a crowded field that has expanded to include natural sweeteners like Splenda and Truvia. There's nothing like a classic.

HISTORY LESSON

My grandpa Benjamin Eisenstadt, a solidly built Brooklyn business owner, was always on a diet. In the 1950s, this meant skipping dessert. In place of sugar, he used cyclamate pills—thirty to fifty times sweeter than sucrose—which he dropped into his coffee. But Ben craved sugar, less for the taste than for the way it felt on the tongue, how it rained into his ice tea. He wondered why, though we had the automobile and the jet plane, there was no good sugar substitute. It gave him an idea, which dovetailed with another. Ben owned a small factory, which he'd converted from a family diner, where, in addition to sugar (Ben also invented the sugar packet, which is another story), he packed soy sauce and coins, but he dreamed of having his own product. In 1956, working with his son, Marvin, as well as a chemist, Ben concocted dozens of versions of fake sugar. When he found just the right mix—saccharine is the main ingredient—he named it after the Tennyson poem "Sweet and Low." Aunt Barbara came up with the design—a musical clef rising toward cost-free exuberance. The pink packet was made to stand out amid a sea of sugar white. Ben started by selling the fake sugar to hospitals and pharmacies as a salve for diabetics and the obese. People were soon turning up at the factory, asking to buy it in bulk. Ben had stumbled upon a truth behind every successful business: it turned out that his desire—to remake himself in the shape of the men on the billboards—was shared by millions of others. He'd plugged into the zeitgeist, which made Sweet'N Low ubiquitous and Ben rich. My branch of the family? Well, the short of it is, I'm not rich. The long of it is my father, who while courting my mother had been used as a lab rat, forced to drink cup after cup of fake sugar, upon learning in 1977 that saccharine possibly caused cancer, muttered to himself, "I knew that son of a bitch was trying to kill me."

Rich Cohen

Teiglach

By Gabriella Gershenson

Every Rosh Hashanah, my grandmother Rhoda, a proud Rigan, boiled knots of dough in honey syrup until they were as golden and shiny as amber, and almost as hard. She'd place each pastry in a cupcake liner, where the remnants of the glaze would drip down and solidify into a chewy foot that could yank out your fillings. These were *teiglach*, as beautiful as they were austere, and a delicacy in my family. You may be more familiar with the teiglach made by Lithuanians, a heap of dough nuggets held together by the sticky glaze they were cooked in, sometimes with nuts or candied fruit thrown in. And if those sound like Italian *struffoli*, you wouldn't be wrong. Teiglach's roots go back to the *vermiculos* of ancient Rome, fried squiggles of dough smothered in honey and seasoned with pepper.

And, like many things Jewish, teiglach's sweet rewards come with the risk of pain. Or, at least, a visit to the dentist.

TEIGLACH

Serves 4 to 6

1 cup plus 1 tablespoon (137 grams) unbleached all-purpose flour, plus more for dusting

⅛ teaspoon salt

2 large eggs

1 teaspoon pure vanilla extract

Zest of ½ orange

Zest of ½ lemon

Canola oil, for frying

½ cup (120 milliliters) honey

⅛ teaspoon freshly ground black pepper (optional)

In the bowl of a stand mixer fitted with the paddle attachment, combine the flour, salt, eggs, ½ teaspoon of the vanilla, the orange zest, and the lemon zest. (You can also combine all these in a large bowl and mix by hand.) Mix on medium-high speed until thoroughly combined, 2 to 3 minutes; the dough will be sticky.

Using flour as needed to prevent the dough from sticking to the counter, turn the dough out onto a work surface. Divide the dough into three roughly equal pieces and roll each into a ½-inch-thick (1.5-centimeter) log.

Cut the logs crosswise into ¼-inch (6-millimeter) nubs using a sharp knife, a bench scraper, or a pair of scissors dusted with flour. Quickly roll the pieces between your fingers to give them a rustic, irregular shape—the crevices and nooks will allow for better glaze adherence. Set aside.

Heat 2 inches (5 centimeters) of canola oil in a large, heavy-bottomed saucepan over medium-high heat until it reaches 350°F (177°C). Line a baking sheet or a bowl with paper towels.

Fry the dough balls in batches, a couple of handfuls at a time, making sure not to overcrowd the pot. Use a slotted spoon or a spider to turn them over as they cook until they are golden brown all over, 45 seconds to 1 minute. Transfer to the paper towel–lined pan or bowl to drain. Repeat to cook the remaining dough balls. Transfer the drained fried dough balls to a large mixing bowl.

Combine the honey, remaining ½ teaspoon vanilla, and the pepper (if using) in a small saucepan. Bring the honey to a simmer over medium-high heat—it will loosen at first and become syrup-like—and cook until it reduces slightly, about 10 minutes. (While the honey is hot, it may not appear to have thickened, but once it cools, it'll have a slightly stiffer body.) Pour the honey over the fried dough balls, tossing them in the syrup with a spoon to coat.

Transfer to a cake platter or a shallow serving bowl and serve immediately.

Tofutti®
BRAND
DAIRY FREE
Tofutti®
BRAND
DAIRY FREE
Tofutti®
BRAND
DAIRY FREE
Tofutti®
BRAND
DAIRY FREE

Tofutti

By Esther Werdiger

Jews made dairy-free ice cream happen, and it wasn't for health or environmental reasons. It was because they wanted to eat a dessert on the Sabbath that wasn't compote (sorry, Mom). I still find it funny when earnest vegans discover pareve food, because while they're making conscious choices, we just wanted to eat what we wanted—all the time.

Tofutti is the poster child for this concept and well predates the surge of dairy-free desserts available today. Tofutti was invented in 1981, after some difficulty, by David Mintz, an Orthodox Jew who was encouraged to persevere by the Lubavitcher Rebbe, a man who clearly understood the importance of a treat that makes it easier to be kosher. With Tofutti's dorky dad humor (butter pecan became "Better Pecan") and Jewish *simcha*-themed packaging (see "Marry Me" ice cream bars), the whole operation strikes me as very haimish. Tofutti Cutie is still a perfect name for an ice cream sandwich, and I could probably pull together a minyan of people anywhere who at some point had a dependency on Tofutti's 30-calorie fudge pops. Mintz also credits his wife, Rachel, with having faith during the arduous process of developing his now famous secret formula, which is my favorite part of the origin story. Because it's hard to decide which is more Jewish: a pareve dessert or a steadfast wife named Rachel.

Treyf

By Liel Leibovitz

For anyone contemplating the laws of kashrut, the decision is inevitably reduced to a crude culinary arithmetic. Consider parting with *treyf*, and, soon enough, you'll find yourself mentally dividing everything edible into three groups.

In the first, entitled "Food I'm Not Likely to Miss," I put shrimp cocktail and fried calamari and ham sandwiches, all of which I have always enjoyed but none of which, I realized, I would ever miss if I resolved to no longer be a few cheeseburgers removed from the faith of my fathers.

Speaking of cheeseburgers, I put them in group number two, "Food I'm Somewhat Likely to Miss," together with the oysters I enjoyed slurping with my dry martinis and the lobster I loved drowning in butter on breezy summer evenings with my family on Cape Cod.

But group number three, reserved for food I absolutely could not imagine living without, contained one single entry: bacon.

It was, after all, my original sin, the instrument of my fall from grace. I had spent the first decade and a half of my life blissfully unaware of its scent or its taste, raised in a kosher home in Israel where a hearty cholent was the peak of fleshy goodness. And then, one day, slogging through puberty, I slouched into a friend's home and smelled something transcendent. I understood, with that one whiff, what it must've been like to stand in the ancient Temple and take in the smoke rising from the burnt offering, every breath making clearer the spiritual affinities between meat and the divine. I asked my friend's mother what she was making, and she replied that it was bacon. She might as well have said Kryptonite: Bacon was a substance I had never imagined actually existed on the same planet I, myself, inhabited. She asked me if I wanted a strip. Without thinking, I said that I did.

Reader, I loved it. The appeal was more than gustatory; it was emotional. Eating bacon was like taking communion in a religion of my choosing, casting off the yoke of tradition my parents had placed on my back without my comprehension or consent. I still believed in God, still felt deeply Jewish, was still proud of my heritage, but with every crispy, fatty bite, I felt I was forging my own path forward, a path that didn't require me to forgo life's pleasures to pledge my allegiance to my people and my faith. I delivered a version of this sermon often, frequently over breakfast buffets where bacon took its rightful place beside the potatoes and next to the eggs.

$\longrightarrow$

When I got older, when the wisdom of old ideas shone brightly and kashrut began to beckon to me, I hesitated for a long time—mainly because of bacon. Giving it up felt like surrender. I was never, I realized, going to rationalize my way into submission. If I was going to return to the purities of my youth, I had to just plunge in and do it.

At first, every meal was a small heartbreak, defined by the meat that wasn't there. Was this burger really good without a strip or two on top? Was that salad really healthy without the gift of crumbled goodness? And, most important, was my spirit growing even as my waist trimmed down?

I got my answer one balmy afternoon as we New Yorkers often do: on the street. I was hurrying somewhere when I passed an outdoor café where a young woman had just received her order: a BLT, the very spiritual balm I had ordered on so many drunken nights. I slowed down, allowing the familiar smell to settle in my nostrils. I expected to feel jittery, angry, distressed. Instead, I felt what might've been the greatest calm of my life. It wasn't the calm of comprehension, since I still can't fully articulate why I decided to once again keep kosher. It was the calm of mastery and of mystery, of knowing that my soul, responding to strange signals from the primordial past, is being called upon to do something it doesn't yet understand and that it can still command the gullet to do its bidding.

By not eating bacon, in other words, I felt at the same time completely in charge and not at all in charge, which is about as good a description of life as you're likely to find. I still miss bacon, though less every day. Meat is great, but meaning is better.

Tsimmes

By Michael Wex

The funny-sounding name comes from the Middle High German *zuomuese*, which means "side dish"; the contents are defined by the fruits or vegetables available and the cook's imagination. While a mango–passion fruit tsimmes is theoretically possible, the first thing to come into the mind of any native eater of Yiddish food who hears the word *tsimmes* is likely to be a carrot. The carrot tsimmes is to tsimmes what the gin martini is to martinis—the standard to which all others must aspire. Sliced carrots, honey, a nice luminous roux made of flour, schmaltz (page 236), and the liquid from the carrots and honey—when it doesn't spell "Shabbos," it spells "Rosh Hashanah."

→

So where does tropical fruit come in? Far from being newfangled or inauthentic, the canned pineapple prominent in so many a modern tsimmes started out as a token of freedom, stewed proof that the old country was really behind us. Introduced into Russia in the eighteenth century, pineapples were grown in hothouses, usually by members of the aristocracy, and, as food historian Joyce Toomre says, quickly became "a symbol of luxury and Western culture." Exactly. This apparently incongruous addition to one of our oldest traditional dishes was really a tangy fuck-you to the czar and all his policies. Pineapple-happy Jewish immigrants were putting American abundance into the service of a hitherto unrealizable European ideal.

But don't look to tsimmes for political consistency. An upper-class person, one to the manner born, can be described as coming from the tsimmes, much as you'd call the same person a member of the upper crust in English. In Yiddish, as in English, you could also say that he or she is from the same *smetene*, the very cream of society, but only Yiddish can portray Caroline Kennedy as a glistening vegetable stew.

TSIMMES

Serves 4

2 cups plus 2 tablespoons (510 milliliters) cold water

1¼ teaspoons kosher salt, plus more to taste

2 long strips of orange zest (peeled with a vegetable peeler)

6 large carrots (1 pound/455 grams), thick ends split lengthwise, cut crosswise into 1½-inch (4-centimeter) pieces

½ cup (120 milliliters) fresh orange juice

2 tablespoons (30 milliliters) honey, plus more to taste

12 to 15 pitted prunes (¾ cup/165 grams)

2 teaspoons fresh lemon juice

½ teaspoon cornstarch

2 tablespoons (6 grams) finely chopped fresh parsley

Combine 2 cups (480 milliliters) of the water, 1 teaspoon of the salt, and the orange zest in a medium saucepan and bring to a boil over high heat. Add the carrots, bring back to a boil, then reduce the heat to medium. Cover the pot with the lid ajar and simmer until the carrots are soft enough that a sharp knife can go through without resistance, but they still have some bite, about 15 minutes. Remove from the heat, strain the cooking liquid into a bowl, and reserve it. Discard the orange peel and set the carrots aside.

In the same pot, stir together ½ cup (120 milliliters) of the reserved cooking liquid, the orange juice, honey, and the remaining ¼ teaspoon of the salt, then add the carrots. If they are not completely submerged in the liquid, add more of the reserved cooking water. Bring to a boil over high heat, boil for about 3 minutes, then reduce the heat to low. Cover the pot with the lid ajar and simmer until the carrots are very soft, about 30 minutes.

Add the prunes and cook until they are soft but still whole, about 15 minutes more. Add the lemon juice. Taste and add more salt and honey, if needed, to achieve a subtle sweet-and-sour flavor.

Dissolve the cornstarch in the remaining 2 tablespoons (30 milliliters) cold water and add it to the pot. Briefly increase the heat to high to bring the liquid to a boil and cook for 2 to 3 minutes. Carefully stir to coat the carrots and prunes with the thickened liquid.

Transfer the tsimmes to a serving dish and sprinkle with the parsley before serving.

The tsimmes will keep in an airtight container in the refrigerator for 3 to 4 days.

Tuna Fish

By Esther Werdiger

A friend of mine whose young family had outgrown the confines of Brooklyn-apartment living recently bought a house in Pomona, New York. Suspecting I may be a few years behind him on the leaving-the-city timeline, I asked what the Jewish community was like there.

"Well," he answered, "there are Chabadniks, Toonabygels—"

I interrupted and asked, "What is a Toonabygel?"

And he said, "You know, Chassidish people who aren't so Chassidish anymore but they still order a '*toonabygel*'!"

I grew up in a strictly kosher household in Australia; the only thing we'd ever get at a nonkosher restaurant was a drink that came in a sealed bottle. And that drink would have to be on the kosher list, a small and thick book that my mother kept in her handbag.

I'm still quite strict—I genuinely feel a sort of visceral clenching when I hear or read about pork—but I do now patronize regular-person restaurants. That world is still somewhat novel to me. For example: diners! I grew up seeing diners only in movies. To eat at a diner, for me, is a borderline cinematic experience, full of pleasurably borrowed nostalgia. But when the mere mention of *treyf* meat still makes me lose my hearing for a split second, similar to the way I imagine people hear nothing after a bomb explodes, what could I even eat at one of these mythic spots?

$\longrightarrow$

Tuna fish, of course. On toasted rye, which is obviously packaged and probably has an OU certification. And the toaster gets used only to make toast. The tuna itself, from a can, is most certainly certified kosher. Hellmann's mayonnaise, kosher, too. I could win a medal in this kind of mental gymnastics, by the way. But it's the most kosher thing you can order, even in a very *treyf* place. And these are all ingredients you can buy in any supermarket, anywhere in the country. And it's pareve, so you never have to wait.

God bless America. Turns out I'm a Toonabygel, too.

TUNA SALAD

2 (5-ounce/141.7-gram) cans tuna in water, drained

¼ cup plus 2 tablespoons (90 milliliters) mayonnaise

3 tablespoons (30 grams) finely diced red onion (from ½ onion)

2 tablespoons (8 grams) finely chopped fresh parsley

1 tablespoon plus 1 teaspoon (20 milliliters) fresh lemon juice

1 tablespoon (15 milliliters) Dijon mustard

½ teaspoon kosher salt

Freshly ground black pepper

Place the tuna in a medium bowl and mash it with a fork. Add the mayonnaise, onion, parsley, lemon juice, mustard, and salt. Thoroughly combine. Season with pepper. Refrigerate in an airtight container for at least 1 hour or up to overnight before serving. The flavors will deepen after a night in the fridge.

The tuna will keep in an airtight container in the fridge for up to 5 days.

Used Tea Bag

By Wayne Hoffman

One of the most common features of the Jewish kitchen isn't found in a pantry, or a cupboard, or a refrigerator. It's a tea bag—specifically, a used tea bag, air-drying on the counter or creating a tiny puddle on a saucer.

For my parents, who were otherwise coffee drinkers, a cup of tea was a nightly ritual when I was growing up. They didn't go for anything fancy or herbal or decaffeinated; it was Lipton all the way. They'd share a single tea bag between the two of them . . . and then leave it on the counter for the next night. I didn't keep track of how long they'd make it last. It's entirely possible that they had only the one tea bag for my entire childhood.

I've heard similar stories from other Jewish households for decades. Maybe it's a reflection of the ancient Talmudic principle of *bal tashchit*, preventing needless waste, or perhaps it's a more generationally specific tendency among children of the Depression. Growing up poor in Jersey City, my mother (and my aunt) picked this up from my grandmother, who'd lived through the Depression and would never have wasted something as precious as a tea bag.

When I moved away to New York, I kept a small box of Lipton in my cupboard for my parents' annual weekend visits. Once, when my parents and my aunt were all at my apartment, I made them tea, being careful to use one tea bag to make all three cups. But when I tossed the used bag in the garbage afterward, they howled. "It's still good!" they shouted. "You can use it again!"

"I don't drink tea," I protested. (To me, tea tastes exactly how you'd expect: like hot grass clippings.) "I make it only once a year, for you—and you're leaving tomorrow."

They relented, grumbling, but I could almost hear them wondering if it would be so bad to keep the bag on the counter until the next year.

Whitefish Salad

By Tom Colicchio

Whitefish salad is the way my wife and I celebrate both of our families' cultures. She is Jewish—we got engaged over a pastrami sandwich at the Second Avenue Deli—and our children are being raised Jewish. I'm Italian, and we eat salt cod, or baccalà, salad, which is close enough.

And come to think of it: When we go to a friend's house for Yom Kippur break-fast, whitefish salad is the one thing I know will be there, but it's always the last to go! It's the redheaded stepchild of lox. But the truth is, I actually prefer it.

WHITEFISH SALAD

Serves 4 to 6

1 pound (455 grams) smoked whitefish, skinned, boned, and flaked

½ cup (120 milliliters) mayonnaise

¼ cup (60 milliliters) sour cream

3 tablespoons (8 grams) finely chopped fresh dill

1 tablespoon plus 1 teaspoon (12 grams) onion powder

1 tablespoon plus 1 teaspoon (20 milliliters) fresh lemon juice

1 tablespoon (15 milliliters) Dijon mustard

Salt and freshly ground black pepper

Shred the whitefish into a large bowl using a fork or your fingers until no large pieces remain, removing any remaining small bones. Add the mayonnaise, sour cream, dill, onion powder, lemon juice, and mustard and use a fork to thoroughly combine. Season with salt and pepper. Cover and refrigerate for at least 1 hour and up to overnight before serving.

Serve with bagels, bialys (page 36), or sliced challah (page 63).

Wine

By Jill Kargman

I love that my people cherish wine enough to make a special carved chalice for it to toast each life-cycle phase. During a circumcision, wine is sipped when the ween is snipped. A bar mitzvah boy drinks as he becomes a man. A bride and groom partake of the cup as they join in holy matrimony. And much is consumed on a visit to the in-laws. So many of our holidays include wine—including our weekly Shabbat and, of course, Passover.

When I was little, long before I drank, I loved chanting the ten plagues and making the droplets on my Seder plate. *Dam! Blood!* That was the first one, and the wine actually looked like it. As the symbolic other nine came down the pike, I remember trying to keep them apart, but eventually my plagues all ran together in a cattle-disease-locusts-and-death-of-the-firstborn red puddle. Later, when the four questions were far in my rearview mirror, I was delighted to actually partake in the guzzling. Speaking of which: Call me a highbrow oenophile (lots of people do), but this chick *loves* Man-ischewitz. When I drink it, I imagine douchey NorCal sommeliers dramatically swirling it in a glass, noting the tremendous nose of flamboyant cherry-kissed red oak: "This jammy table wine has top notes of Concord grape and . . . Robitussin." Kind of a lot for Jews to pound four glasses of the stuff, but God commanded us to, so *l'chaim*!

(DRUNKEN) HISTORY LESSON

"When the wise man drinks wine, he drinks only enough to accompany the food in his innards. Anyone who becomes drunk is a sinner, is disgraced, and loses his wisdom. And if he becomes inebriated before the unlearned, he has desecrated the Divine Name. It is forbidden to drink in the afternoon, even a small amount, except as part of a meal, as drink which accompanies a meal does not intoxicate. Thus, scholars are only careful to refrain from wine after the meal."

These words of warning come to us courtesy of Maimonides. And as much as we revere the wise rabbi, permit us to raise a toast in defiance: We Jews are the people who drink.

It says so right in the Talmud, which teaches us, in Tractate Pesachim, that "there is no joy but that which is accompanied by wine." Wine, Psalm 104 adds, gladdens the heart. On Passover, we're commanded four cups of it; on Purim, many more.

What are we to make of these mixed messages? Should we heed the Rambam and refrain, or imbibe joyfully?

There are many ways to answer this question. You may, for example, consult that awkward story of Lot, his daughters, and their carafe of wine, or that bit about Noah passing out drunk and naked in front of his sons, and conclude that drinking is just a terrible, horrible, no-good idea. But before we put away our shot glasses forever, consider one other bit of rabbinic wisdom. This one comes to us from Midrash Vayikra Rabbah, a rabbinic interpretation of the book of Leviticus. In it, the unimprovably named Rav Aha tells a story of a man who was so fond of wine, he sold many of his assets to pay for a good bottle. His sons, dismayed, were concerned that their father would squander their entire inheritance on a few Merlots, so they waited until he was drunk one day, carried him to the cemetery, and left him there.

Their plan was simple, a Talmudic-era version of Scared Straight: The old man, they hoped, would wake up, find himself among the headstones, and immediately realize he was drinking himself to death. As the old man was beginning to sober up, a caravan passed by the cemetery. As it happened, it was a caravan of wine merchants, carrying some of the world's finest bottles, and when they heard the old man moaning and groaning, they were convinced it was a ghost emerging from the cemetery to haunt them. Spooked, they dropped their cargo and ran away. The old man, stumbling about, rubbed his eyes in disbelief: There, in front of him, were hundreds of the finest bottles money could buy. He drank and drank and drank, and passed out again.

$\longrightarrow$

A few days later, his sons decided to go to the cemetery and check on their father. When they found him awash in fine booze, they were dumbstruck. "Even here your maker did not forsake you and provided you with drink," said one son. "If your maker gives you wine, how can we stop you from drinking?" And so they took the old man home and provided him with the finest reds and whites until the day he died.

Is there a better description of the dynamic of drinking? Wine, it informs us, makes the drinker lose judgment, which, if you've ever gone for that fourth glass, you know to be true. It turns nondrinkers into judgmental jerks, as anyone who has had the misfortune of sharing a dinner with sour teetotalers can attest. And, most crucially, it is, for better or for worse, divine, a mad spirit given us from above, ours to use poorly or well. We can mine our inebriation for inspiration or for madness, just like the gift of life itself.

Yebra

By Michael J. Cohen

A welcome alternative to the dull stuffed grape leaves in congealed goo you see in specialty stores, *yebra* are stuffed with *hashu*—the meat-and-rice mixture commonly used in Syrian dishes—served hot, and bathed in a tangy sauce of caramelized apricots and tamarind concentrate (*oot* or *temerhindi*).

Syrian Jewish cuisine shares much of its repertoire with the native cuisines of the eastern Mediterranean—where anything that can be stuffed will be stuffed. But yebra's fruity-sour sauce distinguishes its provenance as specifically Jewish—likely influenced by Jews who settled in Aleppo from elsewhere, including Persia, where the use of apricots in savory dishes is more prevalent. It soon became a staple of Sabbath and holiday tables, solidifying its place in the Jewish culinary canon.

$\longrightarrow$

YEBRA WITH APRICOT-TAMARIND SAUCE

Serves 6 to 8

FOR THE HASHU

⅓ cup (70 grams) short-grain white rice

1 pound (455 grams) ground beef

1 teaspoon ground allspice

2 tablespoons (30 milliliters) vegetable oil

1 teaspoon ground cinnamon

1 teaspoon kosher salt

¼ teaspoon freshly ground white pepper

1 medium yellow onion, chopped (optional)

1 cup (135 grams) pine nuts (optional)

FOR THE YEBRA

Preserved grape leaves from 1 (2-pound/907-gram) jar (about 65), drained, rinsed, and patted dry, stems trimmed

2 tablespoons (30 milliliters) vegetable oil

10 ounces (285 grams) dried apricots (not unsulfured)

6 tablespoons (90 milliliters) tamarind concentrate

¼ cup (60 milliliters) fresh lemon juice, plus more to taste

1 tablespoon (15 grams) kosher salt

Make the hashu: Put the rice in a bowl, add enough water to cover, and soak for about 30 minutes. Drain in a fine-mesh sieve and transfer to a large bowl.

Add the meat, allspice, vegetable oil, cinnamon, salt, pepper, and onion and pine nuts (if using) and stir to combine. Set aside.

Make the yebra: Place a grape leaf on a clean work surface, vein-side up—choose larger-size leaves or, if you have many small ones, you can double them up. Place 1 heaping teaspoon of the hashu in the center of the leaf, near the stem edge. Roll the leaf end to end, starting from the stem edge, and fold the sides of the leaf toward the center as you roll. The rolled leaf should resemble a small cigar, about 2½ inches (6 centimeters) long. If you're working with small leaves, your rolls will be shorter. Be sure to eyeball and adjust the amount of filling if you're working with smaller leaves to make the rolling easier. Set the roll aside and repeat with the remaining leaves and filling. (At this point, the rolls can be frozen on a baking sheet lined with waxed paper until solid, then transferred to an airtight container and frozen for up to 1 month.)

Drizzle the oil into a medium saucepan. Place the filled grape leaves and the apricots in the pot, alternating between the two. If you run out of apricots, that's OK—just nestle the rolls next to the apricots so the distribution is more or less even. Cover and cook the rolls over low heat until they begin to sweat, 5 to 8 minutes. Drizzle the tamarind concentrate over the grape leaves. Add the lemon juice and salt. Fill the pan with enough water to come three-quarters of the way up the sides of the rolls and weigh them down with a heatproof plate to prevent them from unraveling. (If the rolls are snug enough in the pan, you can omit the plate.) Raise the heat to medium-high, cover, and bring to a boil, about 3 minutes. Reduce the heat to low and simmer, covered, for 35 to 40 minutes. (Alternatively, place the pan in a preheated 350°F/177°C oven and bake, covered, for 1 hour.) Spoon the cooking liquid over the rolls from time to time. When they are done, the rolls should be neither soupy nor dry; a moderate amount of reduced pan juices should surround them. To minimize tearing, turn the rolls and pan juices onto a serving platter without handling any of them individually.

Yemenite Breads

By Leah Koenig

As a community with limited resources, Yemenite Jews mastered the art of transforming the simple ingredients of fat, flour, and water into a repertoire of glorious baked goods. This resource-fulness, a mark of great Jewish home cooks across cultures, has resulted in tempting everyday breads—like flaky fried *malawach*—as well as a host of decadent Sabbath breads. There's *kubaneh*, a pull-apart centerpiece that's as rich as brioche with a deep brown exterior, and *jachnun*, a crepelike pastry made from dough that gets stretched ultrathin, smeared with clarified butter, then folded and rolled endlessly onto itself. Both are baked overnight at very low temperatures and emerge from the oven downy and caramelized. They're traditionally served after synagogue on Saturday mornings, paired with hard-boiled eggs, a fenugreek condiment called *hilbe*, grated tomatoes, and *schug*, the Yemenite cilantro-chile hot sauce. The dips certainly brighten things up, but a carb-induced Shabbat nap is all but guaranteed to follow—another mark of a Jewish-cooking success.

KUBANEH
by Uri Scheft

Makes one 9-inch (23-centimeter) round loaf

1¼ cups (300 milliliters) cool room-temperature water

2½ tablespoons (20 grams) fresh yeast, or 2¼ teaspoons active dry yeast

4 cups (500 grams) unbleached all-purpose flour, sifted, plus more for shaping

¼ cup (50 grams) sugar

1 tablespoon plus 1 teaspoon (20 grams) fine sea salt

10 tablespoons (1¼ sticks/150 grams), unsalted butter, cut into small pieces

2 ripe tomatoes, grated on the large holes of a box grater

Make the dough: Pour the water into the bowl of a stand mixer fitted with the dough hook. If using fresh yeast, crumble the yeast into the water and use your fingers to rub and dissolve it; if using active dry yeast, whisk the yeast into the water. Add the flour, sugar, and salt.

Mix the dough on low speed to combine the ingredients, stopping the mixer if the dough climbs up the hook or if you need to work in dry ingredients that have settled on the bottom of the bowl. Scrape the bottom and sides of the bowl as needed. Once the dough comes together, increase the speed to medium-high and mix until the dough cleans the bottom and sides of the bowl, about 3 minutes more.

Lightly dust your work surface with a little flour and use a plastic dough scraper to transfer the dough from the mixer bowl to the floured surface. Use your palms to stretch a corner of the dough away from you in one stroke, then fold the front portion over and on top of itself. Give the dough a quarter turn and repeat. Do this about 10 times, until the dough is shaped into a nice smooth round.

Lightly flour a large bowl, set the dough in the bowl, lightly flour the top of the dough, and cover the bowl with plastic wrap. Set it aside at room temperature until it has just about doubled in volume, about 30 minutes (depending on the warmth of the room).

Place the butter in a microwave-safe dish and microwave just until it is very soft and perhaps 25 percent melted, 10 seconds or so. Lightly grease a large plate with a little bit of the butter. Lightly flour your work surface and set the dough on top. Divide it into 8 equal pieces. Cup your hand around a piece of dough, then push and pull it, rolling it against the work surface, to gently shape it into a ball. Set the ball on the buttered plate and repeat with the remaining pieces of dough. Cover the plate with plastic wrap and set it aside at room temperature for 30 minutes.

$\longrightarrow$

Use about 2 tablespoons (30 grams) of the softened butter to generously grease a 9-inch (23-centimeter) springform pan (or use a smaller springform pan or a kubaneh pan). Take about 1 tablespoon of the butter and use it to grease a clean, nonfloured work surface. Take a ball of dough from the plate, smear another tablespoon of the butter on top of it, and gently press and spread it out to form a paper-thin 12- to 13-inch (30- to 33-centimeter) square. Use more butter as needed—you want to use a lot! The butter helps spread the dough very thin without tearing (but don't worry if it tears).

Fold the left side of the dough over the center, then the right side over the left to create a simple fold. Starting at the bottom of the strip, roll the dough into a tight cylinder. Slice the cylinder in half crosswise, then place the halves cut-side up in the prepared springform pan. Repeat with the remaining balls of dough (reserve 1 tablespoon/15 grams of the butter to use when you bake the kubaneh), arranging the pieces in a circle in the pan with a few pieces in the center. If you're using a smaller springform pan or a kubaneh pan, stack the dough (as you would for monkey bread). If you are using a springform pan, wrap the bottom of the pan in a large sheet of aluminum foil just in case any butter drips out (this will prevent the butter from burning and smoking up the oven). If you are using a kubaneh pan, you can skip this step.

Cover the pan with plastic wrap and set it aside in a warm, draft-free place until a finger gently pressed into the dough leaves a depression that quickly fills in by three-quarters, about 40 minutes (depending on how warm the room is).

Preheat the oven to 350°F (177°C).

Melt the remaining 1 tablespoon (15 grams) butter, brush it over the top of the dough, and place the pan in the oven. After 15 minutes, reduce the oven temperature to 325°F (163°C) and bake until the top is deeply golden, 30 to 40 minutes more. Remove the pan from the oven and set it aside to cool for at least 20 minutes before turning the bread out of the pan.

To serve, invert the bread onto a platter so the pretty side faces up. Let people rip the kubaneh apart, separating the bread into small rolls. Serve with grated tomato on the side.

Variation: **Traditional Overnight Kubaneh**

Follow the kubaneh recipe through step 8. Preheat the oven to 225°F (107°C). Set a sheet of aluminum foil on your work surface and smear some of the butter in the center of the foil to make a 9-inch (23-centimeter) round. Remove the plastic wrap from the pan and invert the foil over the pan so the buttered area is centered over the dough, then tightly crimp the foil around the top of the pan.

Place the pan in the oven and set a heavy baking sheet on top to ensure that no steam escapes (if using a kubaneh pan, just place the lid on the pan). Bake for 4½ hours. Turn the oven off and leave the bread in the oven until you're ready to serve it.

Warm the bread before serving. To serve, remove the foil (or kubaneh pan lid) and turn out the bread, then invert it onto a platter so the pretty side faces up. Let people rip the kubaneh apart, separating the clusters into small rolls.

Yemenite Soup

By Matthew Fishbane

My father kept cookbooks on his nightstand, because he *read* them—methodically penciling notes in the index. A simple "T" marked the recipes he wanted to try. After making the dish, he would replace the "T" with a checkmark and rate the result according to his personal scale, from "good" to "excellent" to "superb," with half-marks indicated by an underline and, on rare occasions, a double underline. If a recipe lacked a "T," that meant it was either too much trouble for the imagined result or the ingredients were too hard to find or prohibitively expensive.

Reading cookbooks takes a special imaginative talent. To do it well, you need experience with basic kitchen techniques and their effects on food and a sensorial library of flavors, such that you can conjure what a recipe might deliver from just the words on the page. I have a theory that Diaspora Jews are especially good at it, for obvious reasons. There's also something Talmudic about reading nonnarrative tomes for the pragmatism and mental discipline of it. I thought it strange, until I started cooking.

Reading recipes is how I came to make Joan Nathan's version of Yemenite chicken soup. At first blush, it looks daunting, and I imagine many a novice has shied away. Chicken soup, so complicated? But once you break it down and come to understand it as a basic poultry stock with a spice mixture (*hawaij*), a hot sauce (*schug*), and a mild, medicinal thickener of fenugreek paste (*hilbe*), it blossoms into an alluring temptation. It's chicken soup, that bland emblem of our grubbier European past, "separated from the mainstream of Judaism for at least 2,000 years," as Nathan wrote, where it never lost its bite. The flavorful additives are things Yemeni Jews (and Yemenis) would have at hand in their kitchens, but for me, they were genuinely new combinations to discover. Caraway, cumin, coriander, cardamom, turmeric, saffron, black pepper: the dusty red-ochre colors of a woven rug; smells of the spice trade; Greco-Arabic etymologies. Fenugreek—"mentioned in the Bible," as Nathan points out—what the hell is that anyway? I brought out my mortar and pestle and set to grinding.

And here's the thing: My reading of this recipe was right. That doesn't mean I knew what it would taste like before I made it. It means I could channel my learning and experience of hundreds of chicken soups, Jewish and otherwise, to recognize that this recipe would be good. And it was. It's the brightest, richest, clearest, most fragrant chicken soup I've ever made. My father would label it *superb*.

→

YEMENITE OXTAIL SOUP

Serves 8 to 10

3 pounds (1.4 kilograms) oxtails

2 large onions, coarsely chopped

1 head garlic, cloves peeled and left whole

1 large tomato, almost quartered but not cut all the way through

2 celery stalks, with leaves

1 tablespoon (15 grams) kosher salt, or to taste

1 to 2 tablespoons (7 to 14 grams) hawaij (recipe follows)

4 medium carrots, sliced into ¼-inch-thick (6-millimeter) rounds

4 potatoes (2 pounds/900 grams), peeled and cut into ½-inch (1.5-centimeter) cubes

½ bunch parsley, finely chopped

½ bunch dill, finely chopped

½ bunch cilantro, finely chopped

Cooked rice, for serving (optional)

Harissa, homemade (recipe follows) or store-bought, for serving

---

Put the oxtails in a large stockpot and cover with cold water by about 3 inches (7.5 centimeters). Bring to a boil, skimming off any gray scum that forms on the surface, then reduce the heat so the liquid is at a simmer and cook, uncovered, for 30 minutes.

Add the onions, garlic, tomato, celery, salt, and 1 tablespoon (7 grams) of the hawaij. Cover and simmer until the oxtails are tender, about 3 hours.

Add the carrots, potatoes, and all but 2 tablespoons (6 grams) each of the parsley, dill, and cilantro. Simmer until the vegetables are cooked through, about 10 minutes.

Let the soup cool, then cover and refrigerate overnight to serve the next day, as the rest in the refrigerator really melds the flavors together. Skim off the layer of fat that solidifies on top before reheating.

Serve over rice, if you want, with the remaining 1 tablespoon (7 grams) hawaij stirred in, and with harissa spooned over the top or served in a bowl on the side.

This soup freezes beautifully—store it in an airtight container in the freezer for up to 3 months.

HAWAIJ

2 tablespoons (18 grams) whole black peppercorns

1 tablespoon (8 grams) nigella seeds

1 teaspoon cumin seeds

1 teaspoon coriander seeds

1 teaspoon green cardamom pods, peeled

2 teaspoons ground turmeric

Pinch of saffron (optional)

Either pound the spices in a mortar using a pestle, or use a coffee grinder or small food processor to process the spices until finely ground. Transfer to an airtight container and store in a cool, dark place for up to 2 months.

HARISSA

7 dried chiles de árbol

1 dried guajillo chile

Boiling water, as needed

1 teaspoon red chile flakes

1½ teaspoons cumin seeds

1 teaspoon coriander seeds

1 large garlic clove, smashed

2 tablespoons (30 milliliters) tomato paste

2 teaspoons red wine vinegar

½ teaspoon smoked sweet paprika

1 teaspoon kosher salt

¼ cup plus 1 tablespoon (75 milliliters) extra-virgin olive oil

Place the árbol and guajillo chiles in a large heatproof bowl and add boiling water to cover. Cover with a plate and let sit for about 20 minutes, until the chiles are pliable and cool enough to handle. Drain the chiles and discard the stems and seeds (you may want to wear disposable gloves to do this). Transfer the drained chiles to the bowl of a food processor.

Toast the chili flakes, cumin, and coriander in a small, dry skillet over low heat until fragrant, about 4 minutes. Add to the chiles in the food processor, then add the garlic and pulse until coarsely ground. Add the tomato paste, vinegar, paprika, and salt and process until the mixture is mostly smooth. With the motor running, add ¼ cup (60 milliliters) of the olive oil and process until a smooth paste forms and the oil is incorporated. Transfer the harissa to a jar and cover with the remaining 1 tablespoon (15 milliliters) oil. Cover and refrigerate for up to 1 month.

CREDITS

Chocolate Babka (page 25): Excerpted from *Breaking Breads* / Copyright © 2016 by Uri Scheft / Used by permission of Artisan, a division of Workman Publishing Co., Inc., New York / All Rights Reserved.

Challah (page 63): Excerpted from *Balaboosta* / Copyright © 2013 by Einat Admony / Used by permission of Artisan, a division of Workman Publishing Co., Inc., New York / All Rights Reserved.

Roast Chicken Stuffed with Lemon and Herbs by Joan Nathan (page 73), was originally printed in *Tablet Magazine*, at tabletmag.com, and is reprinted with permission.

Azerbaijani Eggplant Salad by Joan Nathan (page 103) was originally printed in *Tablet Magazine*, at tabletmag.com, and is reprinted with permission.

Herring illustration (page 136) by Maira Kalman

Hummus (page 143): Excerpted from *Balaboosta* / Copyright © 2013 by Einat Admony / Used by permission of Artisan, a division of Workman Publishing Co., Inc., New York / All Rights Reserved.

Kasha Varnishkes (page 150): From *The Mensch Chef: Or Why Delicious Jewish Food Isn't an Oxymoron*, © 2002 by Mitchell Davis. Used by permission of Clarkson Potter/Publishers, an imprint of the Crown Publishing Group, a division of Penguin Random House LLC. All Rights Reserved.

Labda recipe (page 175) from *The Georgian Feast: The Vibrant Culture and Savory Food of the Republic of Georgia*, by Darra Goldstein, © 2018 by the Regents of the University of California. Published by the University of California Press. Used with permission.

Home-Cured Gravlax (Lox; page 184): Excerpted from *What's a Hostess to Do?* / Copyright © 2013 by Susan Spungen / Used by permission of Artisan, a division of Workman Publishing Co., Inc., New York / All Rights Reserved.

Matzo Ball Soup by Joan Nathan (page 196) was originally printed in *Tablet Magazine*, at tabletmag.com, and is reprinted with permission.

Mufleta (page 208): Excerpted from *Breaking Breads* / Copyright © 2016 by Uri Scheft / Used by permission of Artisan, a division of Workman Publishing Co., Inc., New York / All Rights Reserved.

Flourless Chocolate Cake (Pareve Chocolate; page 213): Excerpted and adapted from *The Haven's Kitchen Cooking School* / Copyright © 2017 by Alison Cayne / Used by permission of Artisan, a division of Workman Publishing Co., Inc., New York / All Rights Reserved.

Mohn Kichlach (Poppy Seeds; page 225) by Stacey Harwood-Lehman: was originally printed in *Tablet Magazine*, at tabletmag.com, and is reprinted with permission.

Latkes (Potatoes; page 227): Excerpted from *The Haven's Kitchen Cooking School* / Copyright © 2017 by Alison Cayne / Used by permission of Artisan, a division of Workman Publishing Co., Inc., New York / All Rights Reserved.

Sabich (page 234), Amba Sauce (page 235), Tahini Sauce (page 235): Excerpted from *Balaboosta* / Copyright © 2013 by Einat Admony / Used by permission of Artisan, a division of Workman Publishing Co., Inc., New York / All Rights Reserved.

Shakshuka (page 242): Excerpted from *Balaboosta* / Copyright © 2013 by Einat Admony / Used by permission of Artisan, a division of Workman Publishing Co., Inc., New York / All Rights Reserved.

The Ultimate Sufganiyot by Joan Nathan (page 256) was originally printed in *Tablet Magazine*, at tabletmag.com, and is reprinted with permission.

Two recipes: "Hashu" (page 282) and "Yebra" (page 282) from *Aromas of Aleppo: The Legendary Cuisine of Syrian Jews* by Poopa Dweck. Copyright © 2007 by Poopa Dweck. Reprinted by permission of HarperCollins Publishing.

Kubaneh (page 285): Excerpted from *Breaking Breads* / Copyright © 2016 by Uri Scheft / Used by permission of Artisan, a division of Workman Publishing Co., Inc., New York / All Rights Reserved.

ABOUT THE CONTRIBUTORS

SHALOM AUSLANDER is the author of *Foreskin's Lament* and the novel *Hope: A Tragedy*.

DAN BARBER is the chef-owner of Blue Hill at Stone Barns in Tarrytown, New York, and Blue Hill in New York City.

TAFFY BRODESSER-AKNER is a features writer for the *New York Times*' Culture and Magazine sections. She is the author of *Fleishman Is in Trouble*.

ACTION BRONSON is the author of *F*ck, That's Delicious: An Annotated Guide to Eating Well*.

MENACHEM BUTLER is a contributing editor at *Tablet*, the program coordinator for Jewish Law Projects at the Julis-Rabinowitz Program on Jewish and Israeli Law at the Harvard Law School, and a coeditor of the *Seforim* blog.

STEPHANIE BUTNICK is deputy editor of *Tablet* and a host of *Unorthodox*, its weekly podcast.

IRIN CARMON is a *New York* magazine senior correspondent and a coauthor of *Notorious RBG: The Life and Times of Ruth Bader Ginsburg*.

MELISSA CLARK is a food columnist for the *New York Times* and the author of *Dinner: Changing the Game*.

MICHAEL J. COHEN is a coauthor of *Aromas of Aleppo: The Legendary Cuisine of Syrian Jews*, winner of a 2008 National Jewish Book Award.

RICH COHEN is the author of ten books, including *Tough Jews* and *The Fish That Ate the Whale*.

TOM COLICCHIO is the head judge on *Top Chef* and chef/owner of Crafted Hospitality.

MITCHELL DAVIS is the author of *The Mensch Chef* and executive vice president of the James Beard Foundation.

RACHEL FIGUEROA DE ZIMMERMAN is a Staten Island–based writer who pretends her food is spicy so she doesn't have to share it.

MATTHEW FISHBANE is a senior editor at *Tablet*.

IAN FRAZIER is a staff writer at *The New Yorker* and the author of *Travels in Siberia*.

PAOLA GAVIN is the author of *Hazana: Jewish Vegetarian Cooking*.

GABRIELLA GERSHENSON is a food writer and editor based in New York and a contributor to the *Wall Street Journal*.

MERISSA NATHAN GERSON is a writer and educator living in Los Angeles.

GABRIELA GESELOWITZ is a writer and the former editor of Jewcy.com.

DAVID GITLITZ and the late **LINDA DAVIDSON** are the authors of *A Drizzle of Honey: The Lives and Recipes of Spain's Secret Jews*.

DARRA GOLDSTEIN is the founding editor of *Gastronomica* and the author of several award-winning cookbooks, including *The Georgian Feast*, recently reissued as a twenty-fifth-anniversary edition.

ELISSA GOLDSTEIN is an Australian writer, digital marketer, and podcast producer based in New York.

ROYA HAKAKIAN, a 2018 Hadassah-Brandeis Fellow, is the author of several books, including *Journey from the Land of No*, about growing up Jewish in revolutionary Iran.

AMANDA HESSER and **MERRILL STUBBS** are the cofounders of Food52.

WAYNE HOFFMAN is executive editor of *Tablet*.

GIL HOVAV is an Israeli food personality and the author of *Candies from Heaven*.

MARJORIE INGALL is a *Tablet* columnist and the author of *Mamaleh Knows Best: What Jewish Mothers Do to Raise Successful, Creative, Empathetic, Independent Children*.

EVE JOCHNOWITZ is a Yiddishist and scholar of Ashkenazi foodways.

MAIRA KALMAN is a writer, illustrator, and designer. Her most recent books are *Sara Berman's Closet* (in collaboration with Alex Kalman) and *Bold & Brave* by Kirsten Gillibrand.

JILL KARGMAN is the creator, writer, producer, and star of Bravo's *Odd Mom Out* and the *New York Times* bestselling author of ten books, most recently *Sprinkle Glitter on My Grave*.

BARBARA KIRSHENBLATT-GIMBLETT is chief curator, Core Exhibition, POLIN Museum of the History of Polish Jews.

LEAH KOENIG is the author of *Modern Jewish Cooking: Recipes & Customs for Today's Kitchen* and *The Little Book of Jewish Appetizers*.

EDWARD LEE is the chef-owner of 610 Magnolia in Louisville, Kentucky, and Succotash in Washington, DC.

LIEL LEIBOVITZ is a senior writer at *Tablet* and a host of *Unorthodox*, its weekly podcast.

JOSHUA MALINA has been an actor for thirty years and a Jew for fifty-three.

MANISHTANA is the pseudonym of Shais Rishon, an Orthodox African American Jewish writer, speaker, rabbi, and author of *Thoughts from a Unicorn*. His latest book is *Ariel Samson, Freelance Rabbi*.

DAPHNE MERKIN is a cultural critic and novelist. She contributes regularly to the *New York Times Book Review* and the *Wall Street Journal* Arts section. Her latest book is a memoir, *This Close to Happy: A Reckoning with Depression*.

JOAN NATHAN is *Tablet*'s food columnist and the author of eleven cookbooks, including *King Solomon's Table: A Culinary Exploration of Jewish Cooking from Around the World*.

ALANA NEWHOUSE is the founder and editor of *Tablet*.

YOTAM OTTOLENGHI is a restaurateur, food writer, and bestselling author. His most recent cookbook is *Ottolenghi Simple*.

SHYRLA PAKULA is an Orthodox Jewish doctor, lactation consultant, mother of seven, and grandmother of many more (*Baruch Hashem ptu ptu ptu*). She lives in Melbourne, Australia.

ZAC POSEN is a fashion designer and the author of *Cooking with Zac: Recipes from Rustic to Refined*.

LARA RABINOVITCH is a specialist in food culture and history. She received her PhD from New York University and is a writer and producer in Los Angeles.

RÁCHEL RAJ is a pastry chef, café owner, and daughter of Hungary's onetime chief rabbi. Her award-winning *flódni* is widely regarded as Budapest's finest.

RUTH REICHL is the author of *My Kitchen Year: 136 Recipes That Saved My Life.*

ÉRIC RIPERT is the chef and co-owner of the New York restaurant Le Bernardin.

YAIR ROSENBERG is a senior writer at *Tablet.*

PHIL ROSENTHAL is the creator of *Everybody Loves Raymond* and the host of Netflix's *Somebody Feed Phil.*

DAVID SAMUELS is a writer. He lives with his wife and children in New York.

MARCUS SAMUELSSON is chef-owner of Red Rooster in New York City.

GABRIEL SANDERS is *Tablet*'s director of business development.

DAVID SAX is the author of *Save the Deli: In Search of Perfect Pastrami, Crusty Rye, and the Heart of Jewish Delicatessen.*

ROSIE SCHAAP is the author of *Drinking with Men: A Memoir.*

LIOR LEV SERCARZ is the owner of La Boîte in New York City.

MIMI SHERATON is the author of *The Bialy Eaters* and *1,000 Foods to Eat Before You Die.*

DANYA SHULTS is the founder of Arq, a lifestyle brand and community that helps people connect with Judaism in a relevant, inclusive, convenient way.

GAIL SIMMONS is a judge on *Top Chef* and the author of *Bringing It Home: Favorite Recipes from a Life of Adventurous Eating.*

MICHAEL SOLOMONOV is a chef and cookbook author, and the owner of multiple restaurants, including Zahav, in Philadelphia.

GABRIEL STULMAN is the founder of Happy Cooking Hospitality.

ADINA STEIMAN is a James Beard Award–winning food writer, editor, and digital strategist who's still afraid to try kishke.

ADEENA SUSSMAN is a *New York Times* bestselling cookbook author based in Tel Aviv.

SHIRA TELUSHKIN is a writer based in New York and a producer of Tablet's *Unorthodox* podcast.

MARC TRACY, a *Tablet* staff writer from 2009 to 2012, covers college sports for the *New York Times*.

MICHAEL TWITTY is the author of *The Cooking Gene: A Journey Through African American Culinary History in the Old South*, which won the 2018 James Beard Award for best food writing and book of the year.

CAROL UNGAR is the author of *Jewish Soul Food: Traditional Fare and What It Means*.

KATHARINE WEBER is the author of several books, including *True Confections*.

ESTHER WERDIGER, *Tablet*'s art director, is a writer and artist from Melbourne, Australia.

DR. RUTH WESTHEIMER is a psychosexual therapist, author of more than forty books, and teacher.

MICHAEL WEX is the bestselling author of *Born to Kvetch*.

BEN WIZNER is a longtime ACLU lawyer who prefers his martinis with three olives.

MOLLY YEH is the author of *Molly on the Range* and the host of Food Network's *Girl Meets Farm*.

JEFFREY YOSKOWITZ is the author of *The Gefilte Manifesto: New Recipes for Old World Jewish Foods*.

ALAN ZEITLIN is a journalist living in Manhattan.

LEA ZELTSERMAN was born in St. Petersburg when it was Leningrad, was raised in Alberta, Canada, and now lives in Toronto. She writes about food, books, technology, and Russian-Jewish issues and culture.

ACKNOWLEDGMENTS

This book, like every good recipe, is the product of many hands. If you count the contributions made by colleagues from around the world, friends, family members, even ancestors—and you should—you'll understand that it's truly impossible to properly acknowledge everyone to whom we owe a debt.

To create and animate the original Tablet project, we worked with the dreamiest of dream teams: Gabriella Gershenson (project editor), Victoria Granof (food stylist), Noah Fecks (photographer), and Randi Brookman Harris (prop stylist). That process would never have been the success it was had it not also been for Emma Davis, Niki Russ Federman and Josh Russ Tupper of Russ & Daughters, Parker Feierbach, Elissa Goldstein, Echo Hopkins, Alex Puciarelli, Krystal Rack, Jen Snow, Rachael Weiner, and the hospitality of Noho Studios. We also owe debts to Einat Admony, Stacey Harwood-Lehman, Peter Shelsky, Adeena Sussman, and the late Gil Marks.

We are also grateful to the professional balaboostas who developed the bulk of the recipes for this epic compilation, and brought their iconic flavors to life: Mira Evnine, Anna Gershenson, Rebecca Flint Marx, Olga Massov, and Molly Yeh. A special thanks to Liza Chafiian and Jasmine BenJehuda for sharing their family recipe for Persian rice.

Without Mem Bernstein, Arthur Fried, and Morton Landowne, there would be no Tablet at all—and our lives in particular would be substantially less ambitious and less colorful.

Joan Nathan is our Jewish fairy godmother—and we know exactly how lucky that makes us. We owe Jin Auh at the Wylie Agency piles of lox for the rest of her life.

In Lia Ronnen, Artisan's publisher, we found a person so committed to making smart and beautiful things that to call her kindred almost feels egotistical—and, in turn, Lia put us in the skilled and inspired hands of Judy

Pray and the rest of the team at Artisan. That we found a home with them in the first place is because of Michelle Ishay-Cohen—my chosen family, and the woman at whose table I've literally been eating for decades—who helped us make this book the object of enlightenment and joy that we hope it is for you.

Finally, a note about authorship. The ideas here—from the largest conceptual ones to the smallest details—stem directly from the loud, teeming, at times angry but always loving kitchen that is *Tablet*. I hope we all live to 120 together.

Tablet

EDITOR IN CHIEF: Alana Newhouse

EXECUTIVE EDITOR: Wayne Hoffman

DEPUTY EDITOR: Stephanie Butnick

EDITOR AT LARGE: Mark Oppenheimer

SENIOR EDITOR: Matthew Fishbane

SCROLL EDITOR: Jacob Siegel

SENIOR WRITERS: Liel Leibovitz, Yair Rosenberg

DIRECTOR OF BUSINESS DEVELOPMENT: Gabriel Sanders

ART DIRECTOR: Esther Werdiger

COPY EDITOR: Larry Greenberg

CONTRIBUTING WRITERS: Marjorie Ingall, Armin Rosen

LITERARY EDITOR: David Samuels

CRITIC AT LARGE: Paul Berman

UNORTHODOX PODCAST PRODUCTION: Josh Kross, Shira Telushkin, Noah Levinson, Sophia Steinert-Evoy

INDEX

Alana Newhouse is the editor in chief of *Tablet*, which she founded in 2009. She lives in New York City.